REMNANTS OF THE RED RIBBON SECT

DAWN NELSON-WARDROPE

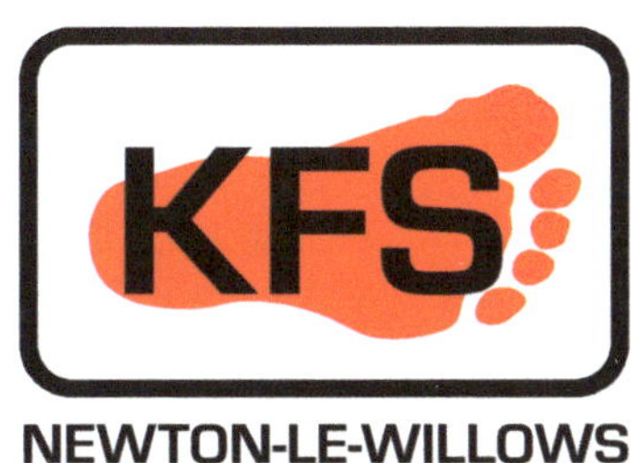

NEWTON-LE-WILLOWS

Merseyside,
WA12 9RG.

ISBN 978-1-912211-38-8

Acknowledgements:

Thanks to Stephen Nelson and Maralena Howard (Artista Daily) for Love and encouragement.

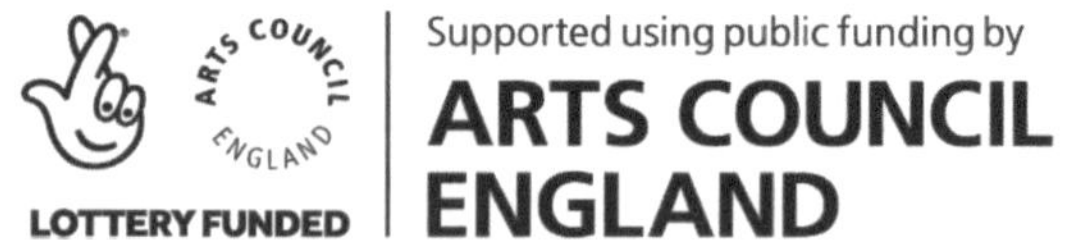

For Sam and Suzi.

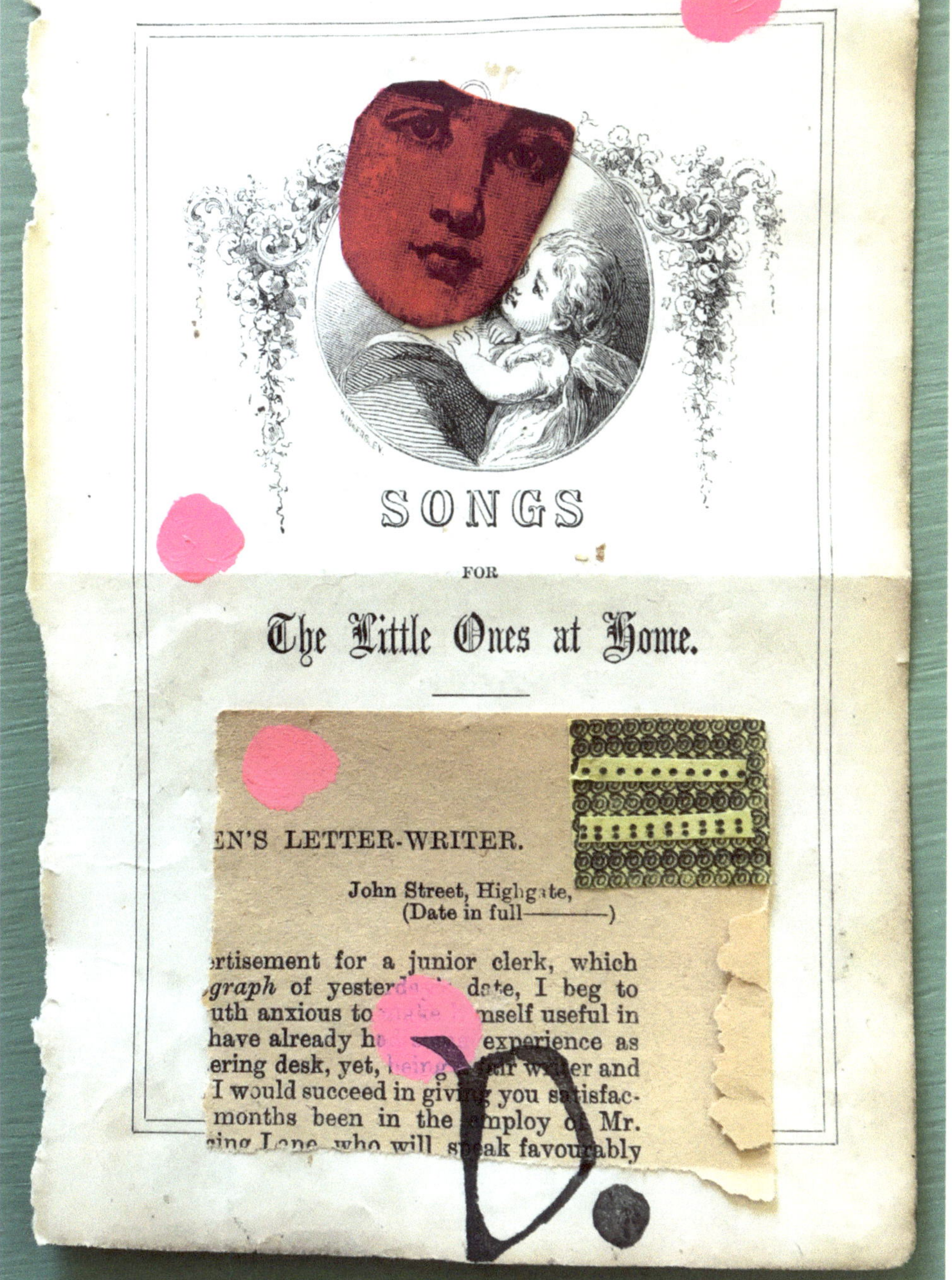

SONGS
FOR
The Little Ones at Home.
EN'S LETTER-WRITER.
John Street, Highgate,
(Date in full————)
ertisement for a junior clerk, which
graph of yesterd
uth anxious to
have already h
ering desk, yet,
I would succeed in giv
months been in the

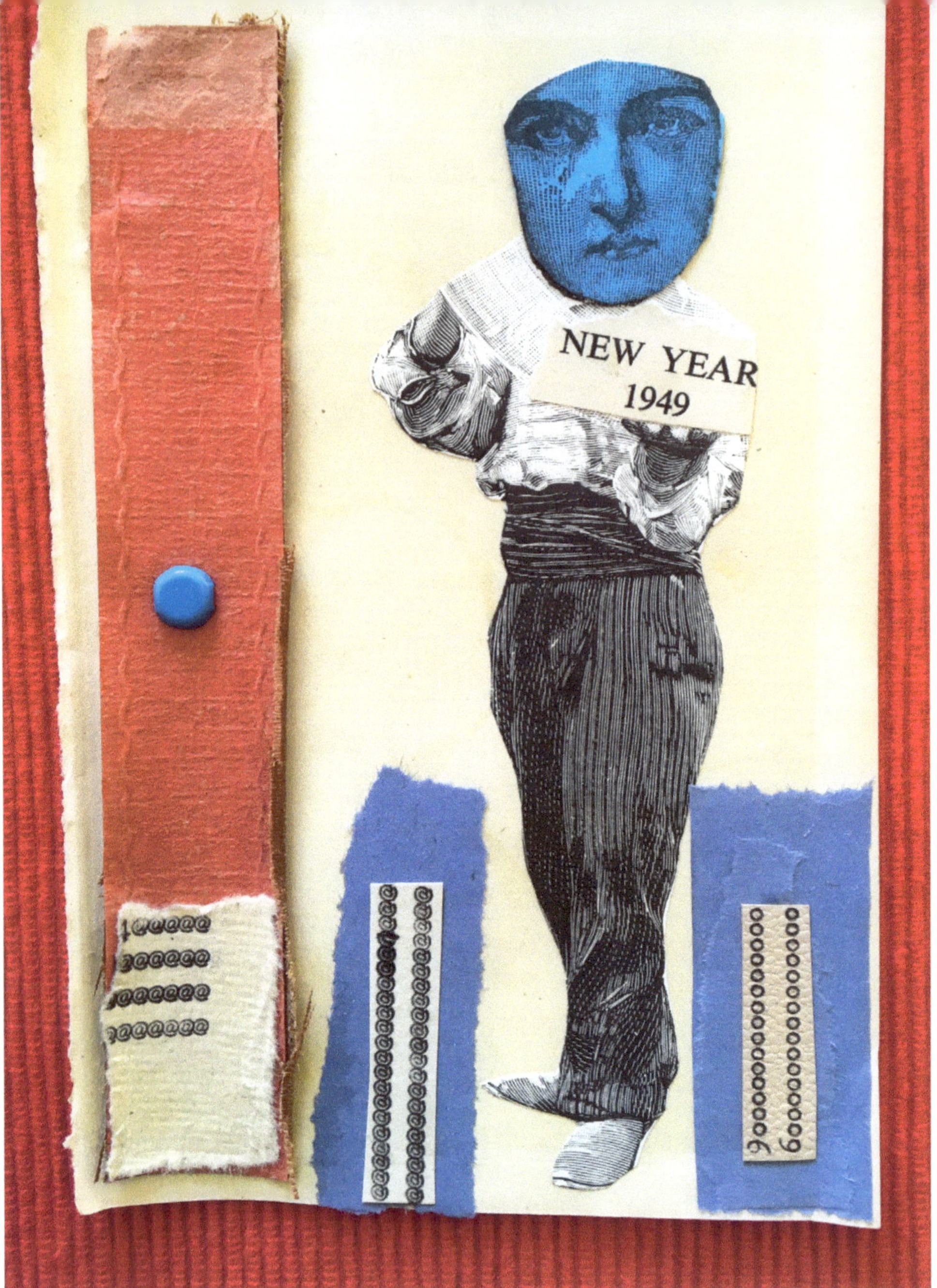
NEW YEAR
1949

THE WINDMILL LIBRARY

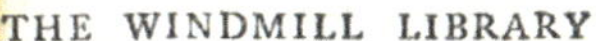

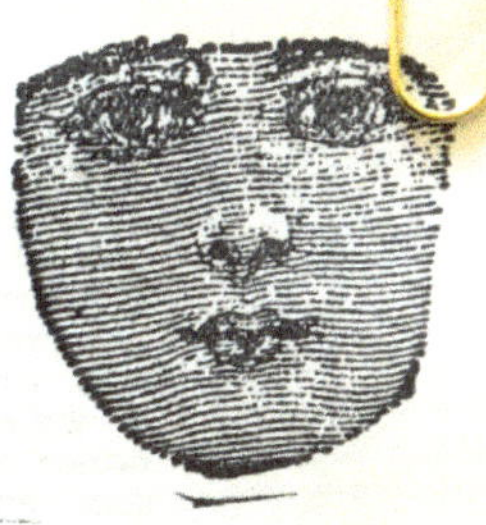

STANDARD BOO 179–9

Second Printing, 1973

C1 2 38 0676161

PP 66620 635/964023

14 MAY 1974

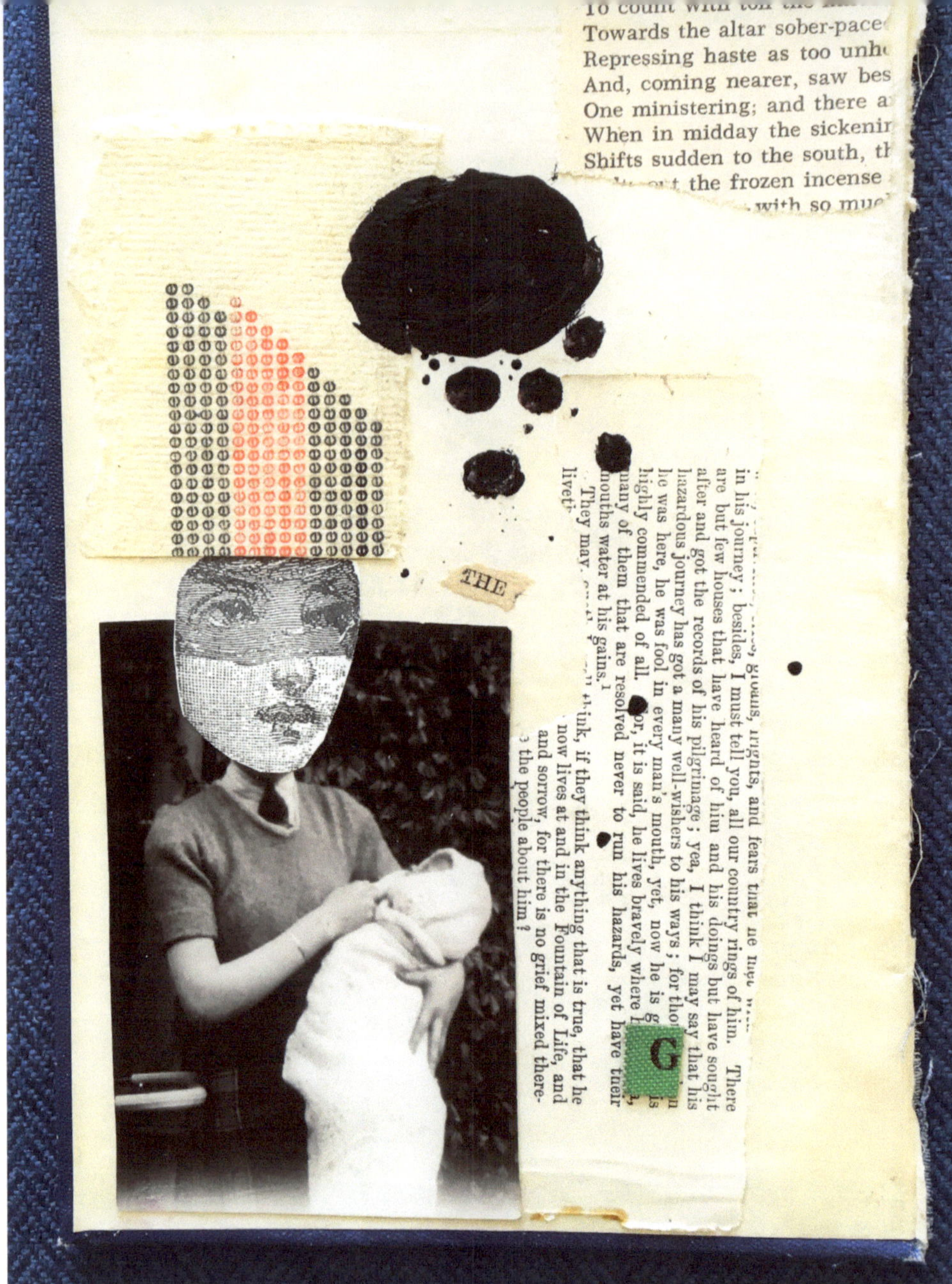
Towards the altar sober-pace
Repressing haste as too unh
And, coming nearer, saw bes
One ministering; and there a
When in midday the sickenir
Shifts sudden to the south, th
the frozen incense
in his journey; besides, I must tell you, all our country rings of him. There
are but few houses that have heard of him and his doings but have sought
after and got the records of his pilgrimage; yea, I think I may say that his
hazardous journey has got a many well-wishers to his ways; for tho
he was here, he was fool in every man's mouth, yet, now he is g
highly commended of all.
many of them that are resolved never to run his hazards, yet have their
mouths water at his gains.
They may
think, if they think anything that is true, that he
now lives at and in the Fountain of Life, and
and sorrow, for there is no grief mixed there-
the people about him?
THE
G

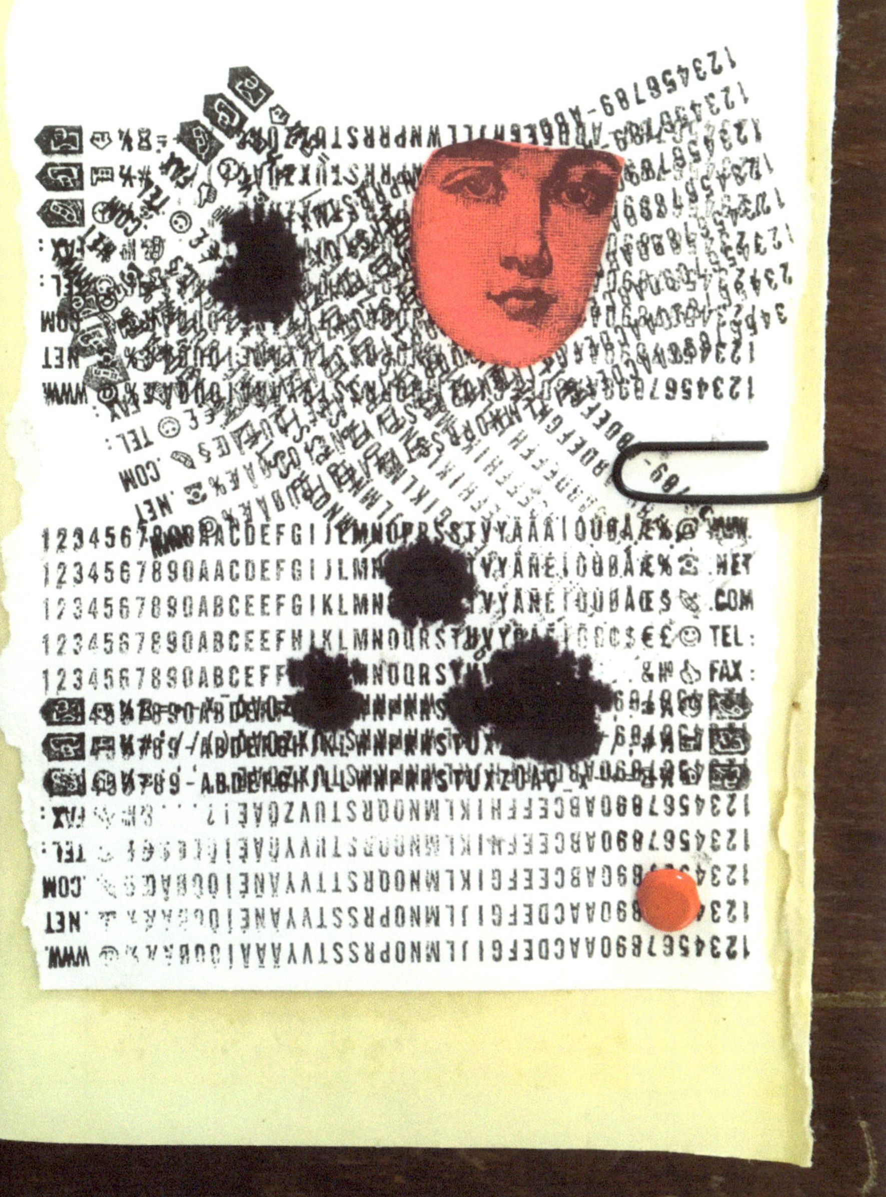

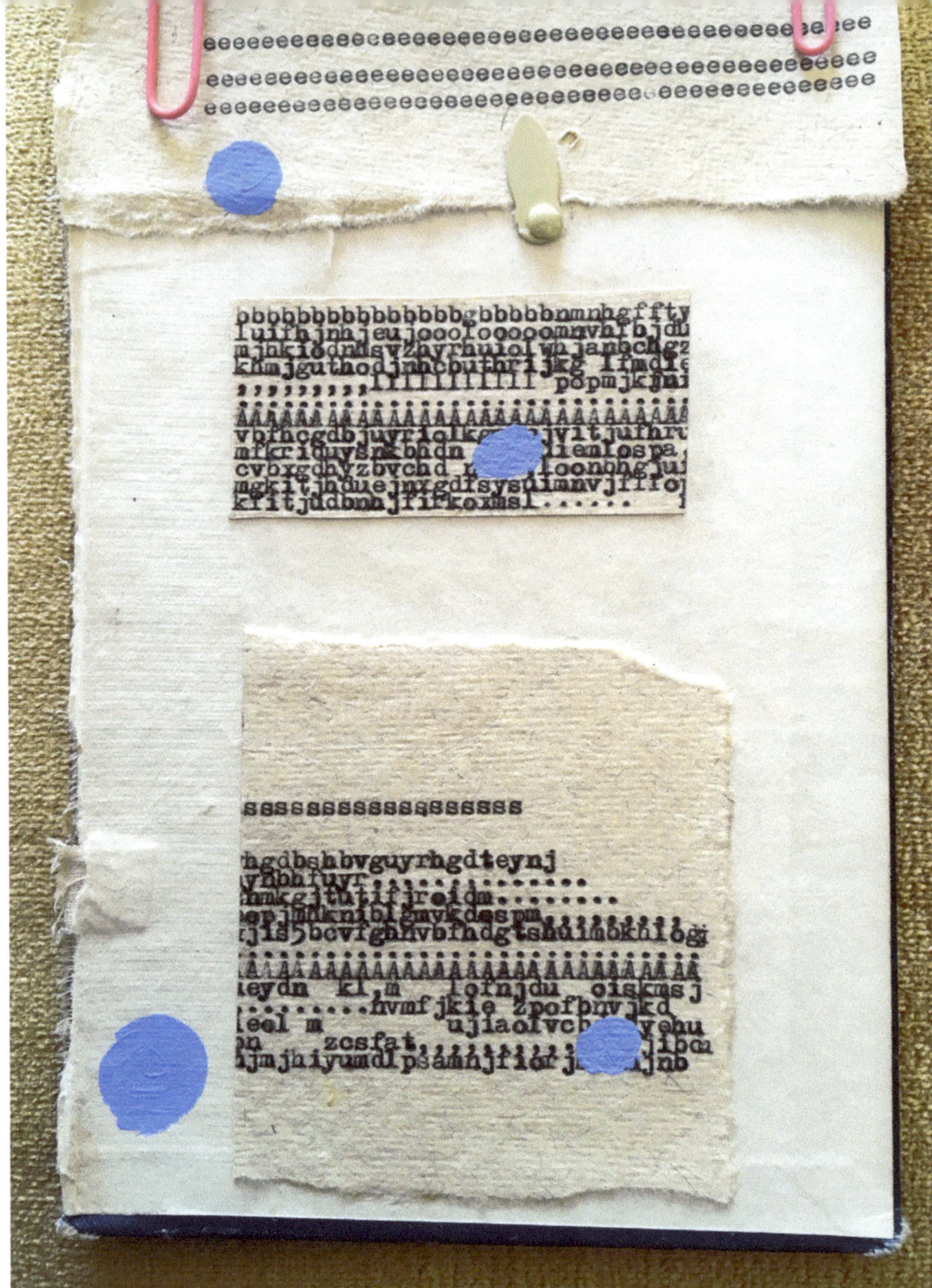

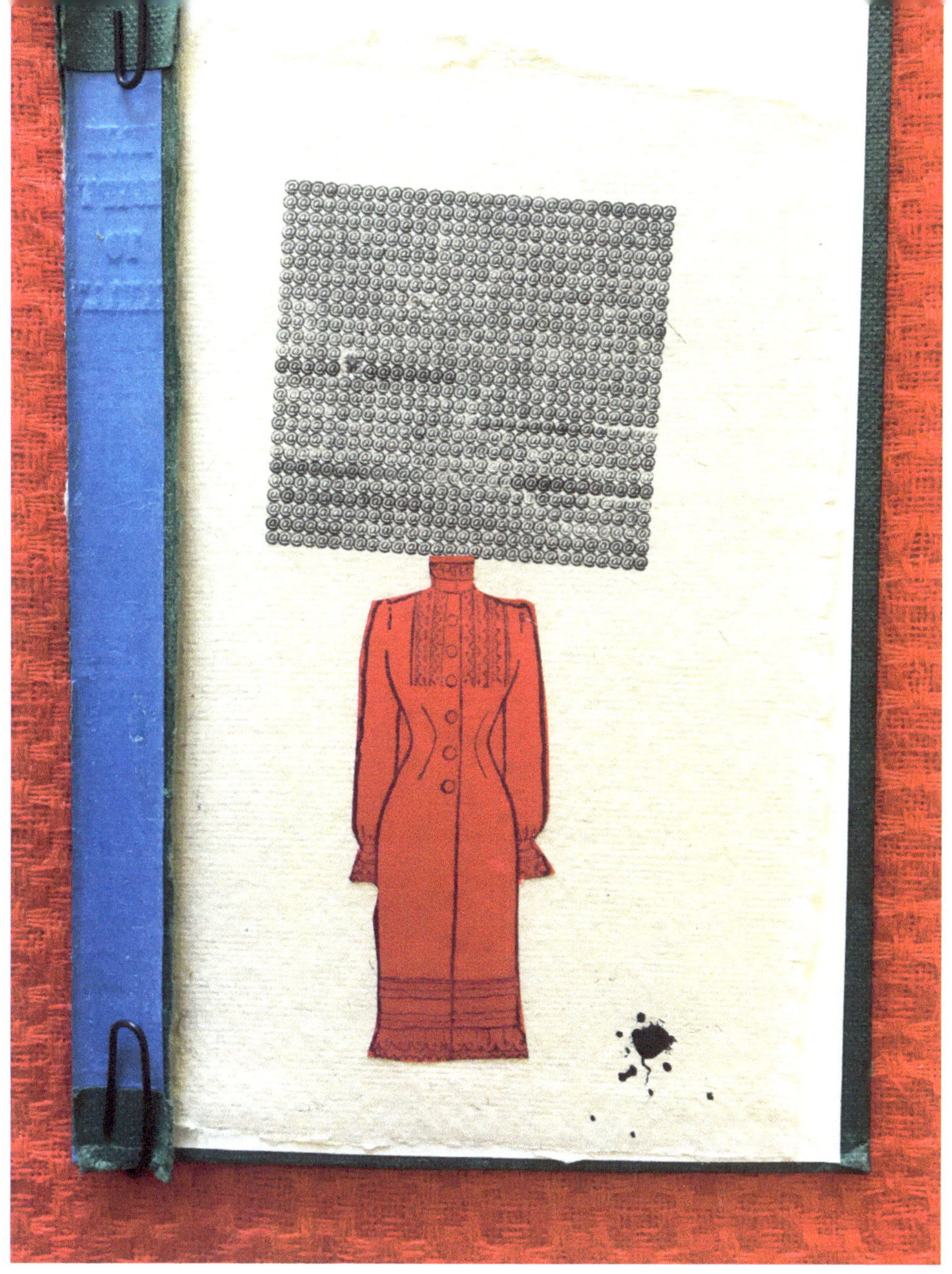

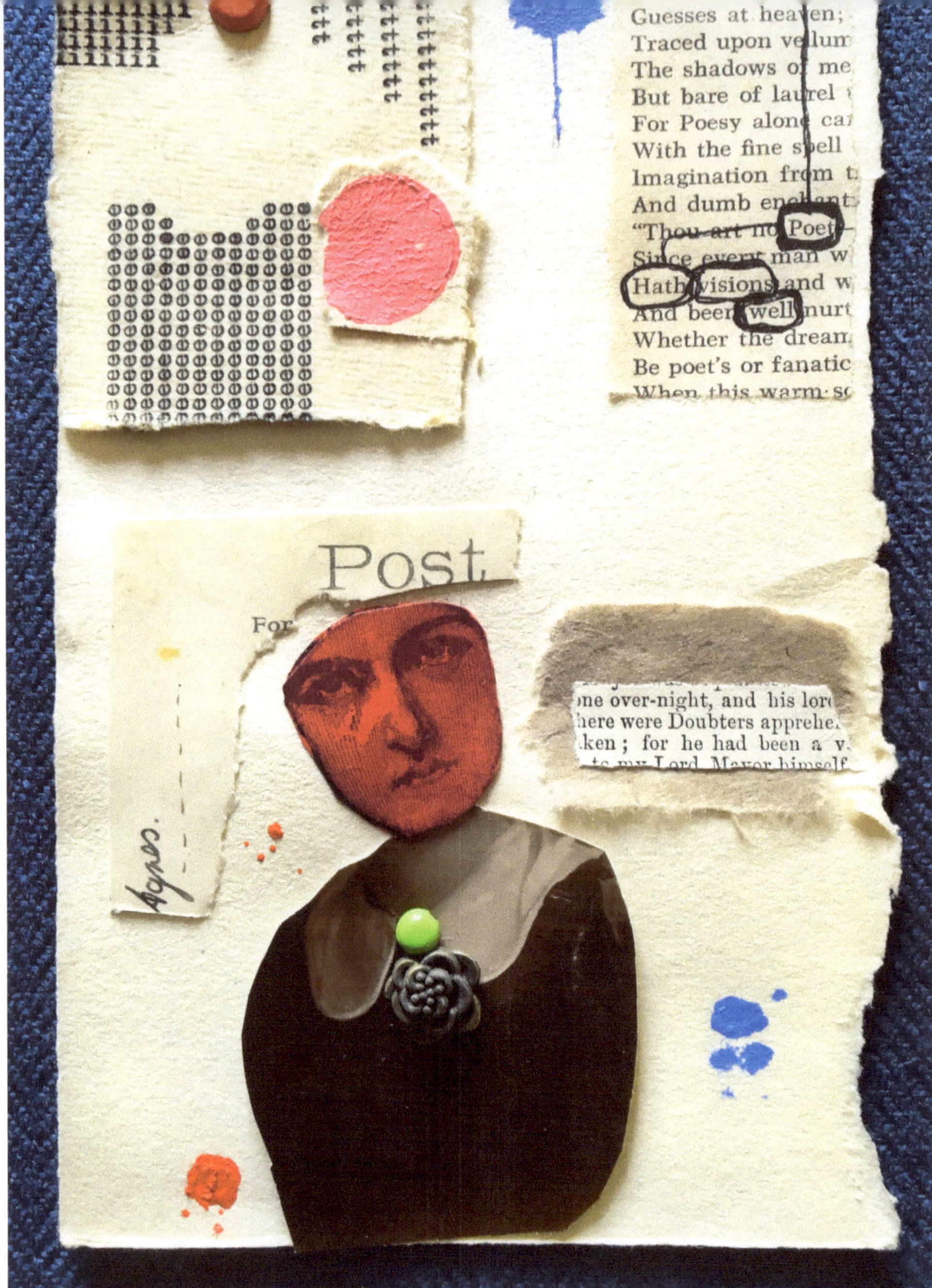

Guesses at heaven;
Traced upon vellum
The shadows of me
But bare of laurel
For Poesy alone
With the fine spell
Imagination from
And dumb enchant
"Thou art no Poet
Since every man w
Hath visions and w
And been well nurt
Whether the dream
Be poet's or fanatic
Post
For
Agnes.
one over-night, and his lord
here were Doubters apprehe
ken; for he had been a

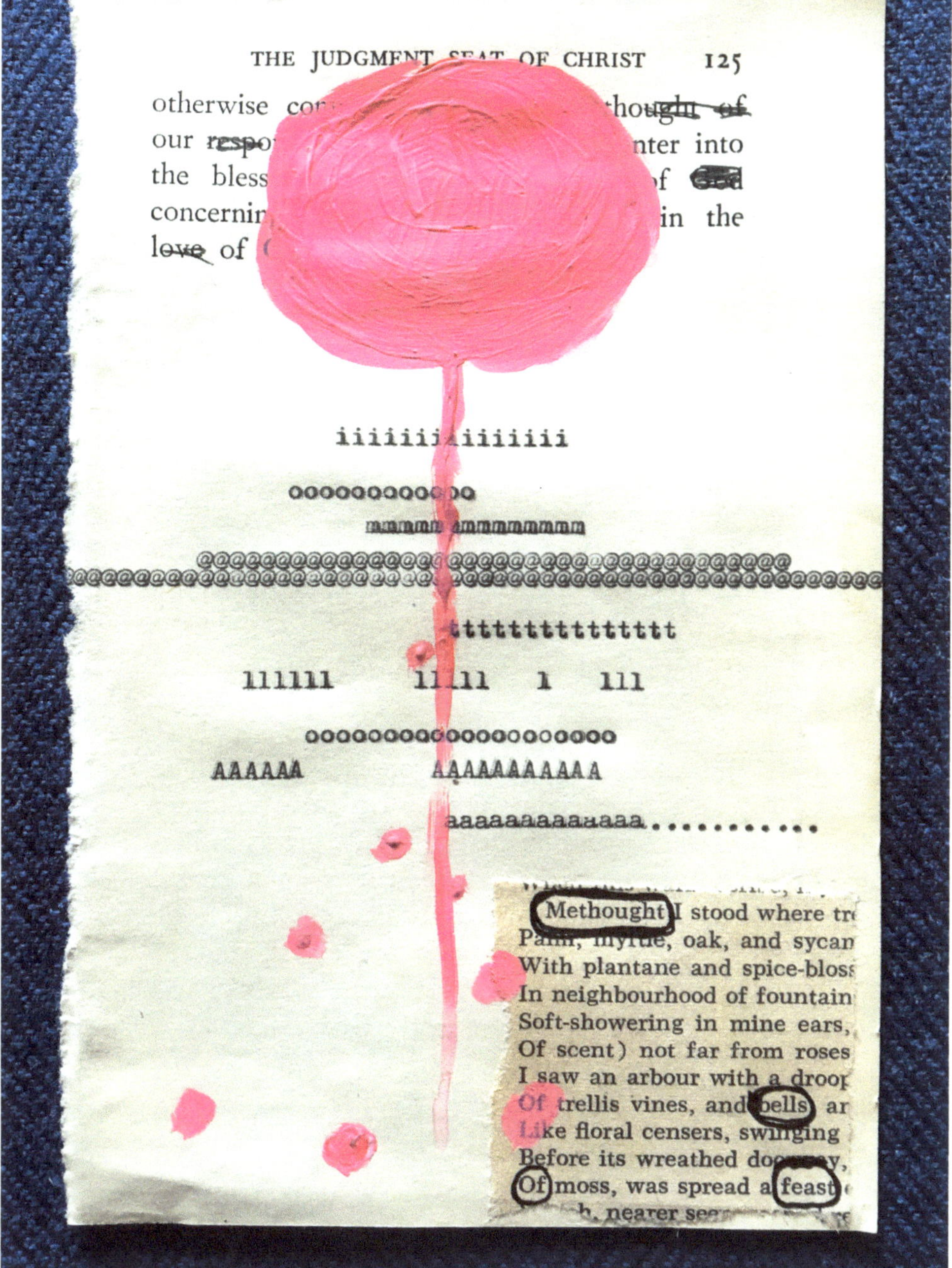
THE JUDGMENT SEAT OF CHRIST 125
iiiiiiiiiiiiii
tttttttttttttt
111111 11111 1 111
AAAAAA AAAAAAAAAAA
aaaaaaaaaaaaa...........
Methought I stood where tr
Palm, myrtle, oak, and sycan
With plantane and spice-bloss
In neighbourhood of fountain
Soft-showering in mine ears,
Of scent) not far from roses
I saw an arbour with a droop
Of trellis vines, and bells ar
Like floral censers, swinging
Before its wreathed doorway,
Of moss, was spread a feast

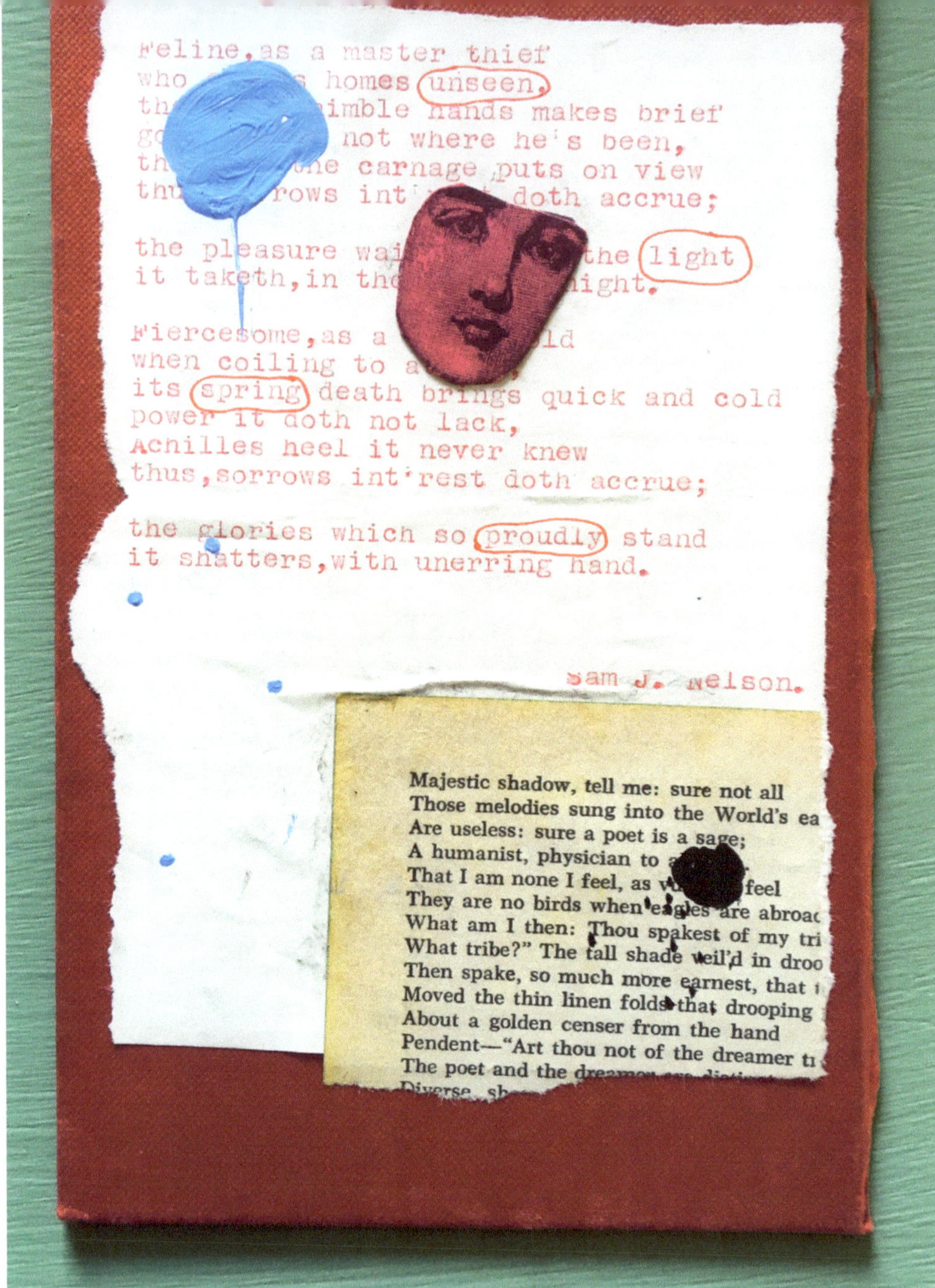
Feline,as a master thief
who homes unseen.
hands makes brief
not where he's been,
carnage puts on view
doth accrue;
the pleasure the light
it taketh,in ight.
Fiercesome,as a
when coiling to
its spring death brings quick and cold
power it doth not lack,
Achilles heel it never knew
thus,sorrows int'rest doth accrue;
the glories which so proudly stand
it shatters,with unerring hand.
Sam J. Nelson.
Majestic shadow, tell me: sure not all
Those melodies sung into the World's ea
Are useless: sure a poet is a sage;
A humanist, physician to
That I am none I feel, as feel
They are no birds when eagles are abroac
What am I then: Thou spakest of my tri
What tribe?" The tall shade veil'd in droo
Then spake, so much more earnest, that
Moved the thin linen folds that drooping
About a golden censer from the hand
Pendent—"Art thou not of the dreamer t
The poet and the

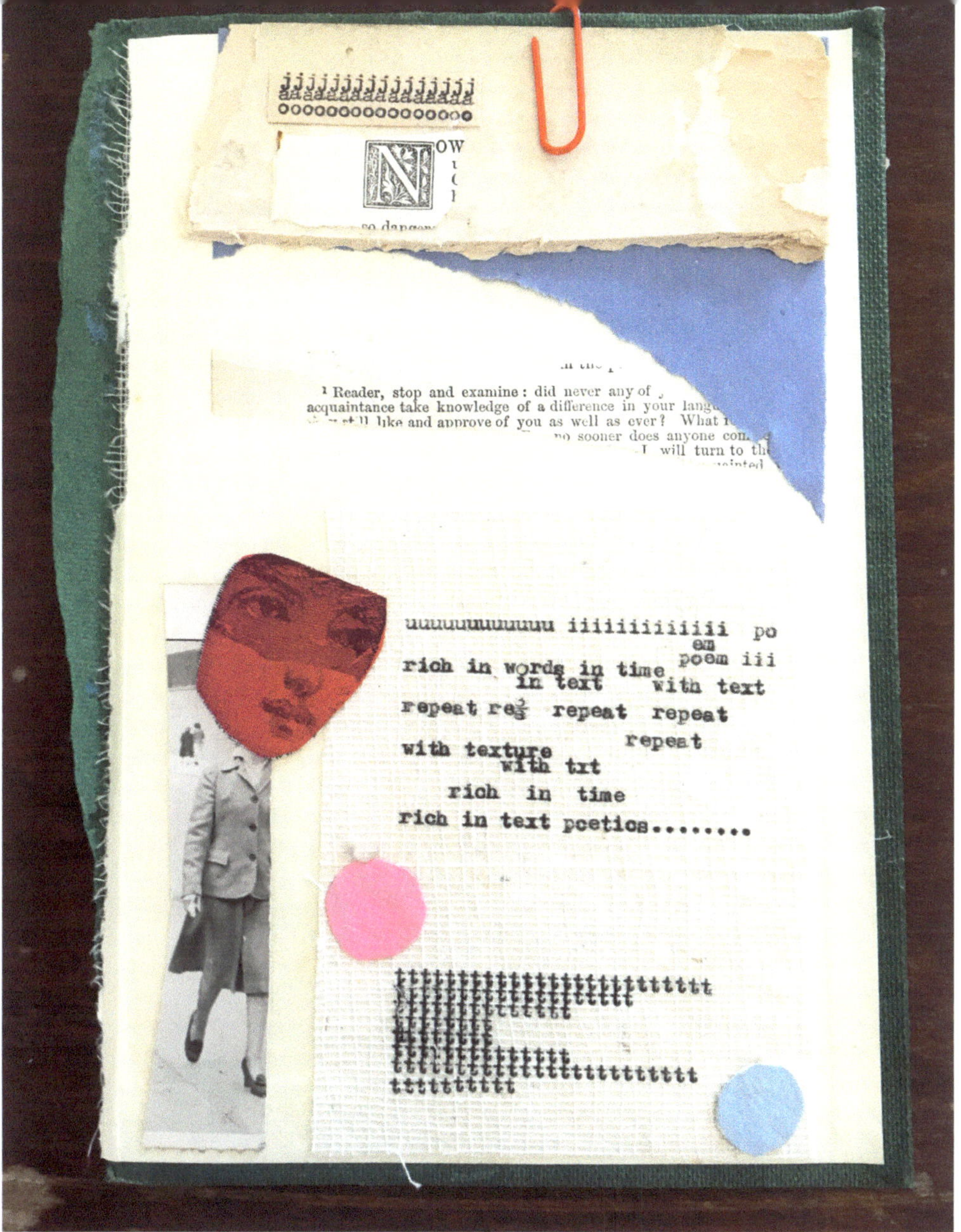
jjjjjjjjjjjjjjjj
aaaaaaaaaaaaaaaa
oooooooooooooooo
¹ Reader, stop and examine : did never any of
acquaintance take knowledge of a difference in your lang
like and approve of you as well as ever? What
no sooner does anyone com
I will turn to th
uuuuuuuuuuuu iiiiiiiiiiii po
em
poem iii
rich in words in time
in text with text
repeat repeat repeat
repeat
with texture
with txt
rich in time
rich in text poetics........

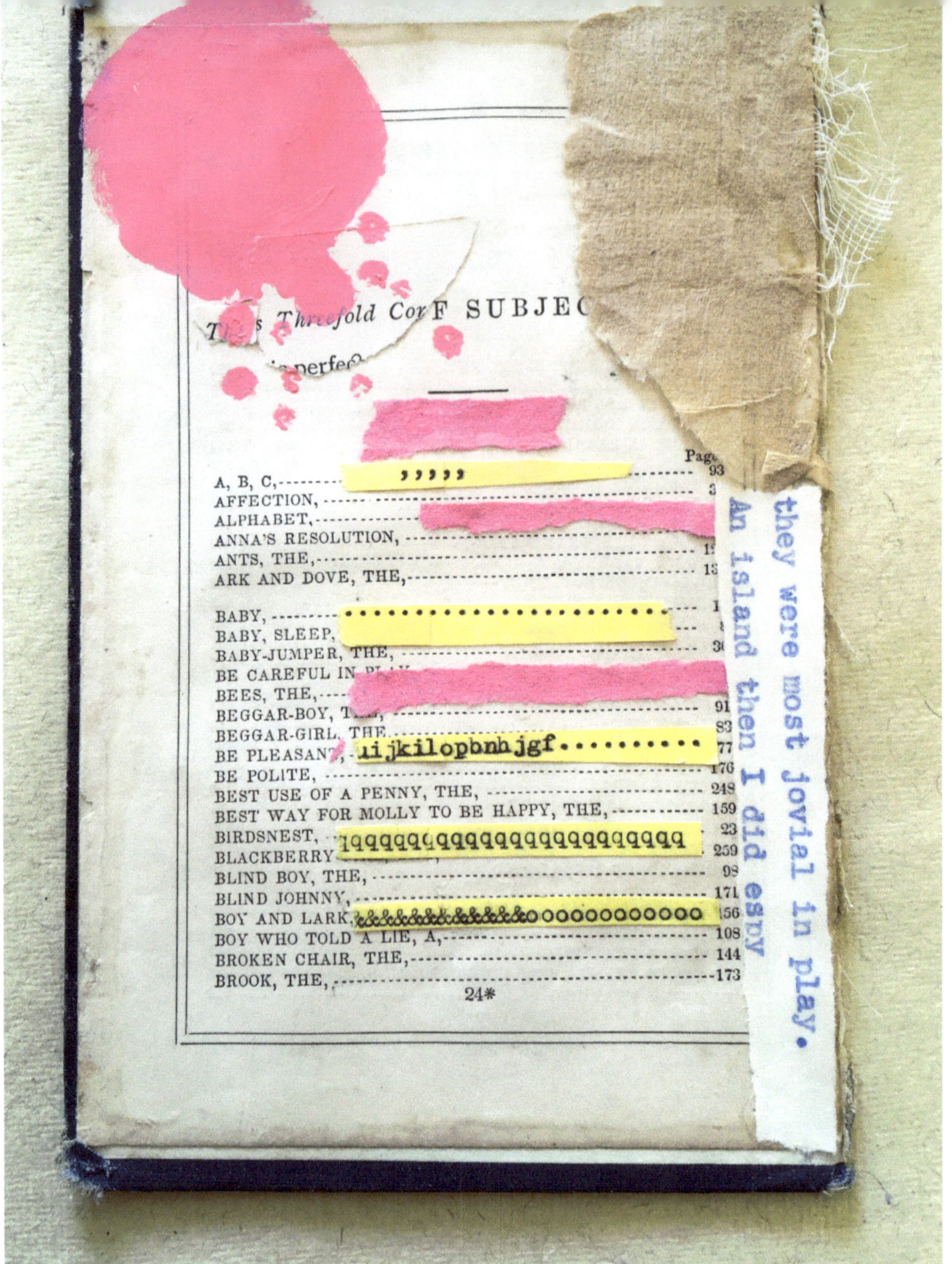
Threefold
F SUBJEC
Page
A, B, C, 93
AFFECTION,
ALPHABET,
ANNA'S RESOLUTION,
ANTS, THE,
ARK AND DOVE, THE,
BABY,
BABY, SLEEP,
BABY-JUMPER, THE,
BE CAREFUL IN
BEES, THE,
BEGGAR-BOY,
BEGGAR-GIRL, THE
BE PLEASANT,
BE POLITE, 176
BEST USE OF A PENNY, THE, 248
BEST WAY FOR MOLLY TO BE HAPPY, THE, 159
BIRDSNEST, 23
BLACKBERRY 259
BLIND BOY, THE, 98
BLIND JOHNNY, 171
BOY AND LARK, 156
BOY WHO TOLD A LIE, A, 108
BROKEN CHAIR, THE, 144
BROOK, THE, 173
24*
ijkilopbnhjgf
qqqqqqqqqqqqqqqqqqqqqqq
&&&&&&&&&&&&&&oooooooooooo
they were most jovial in play.
An island then I did espy

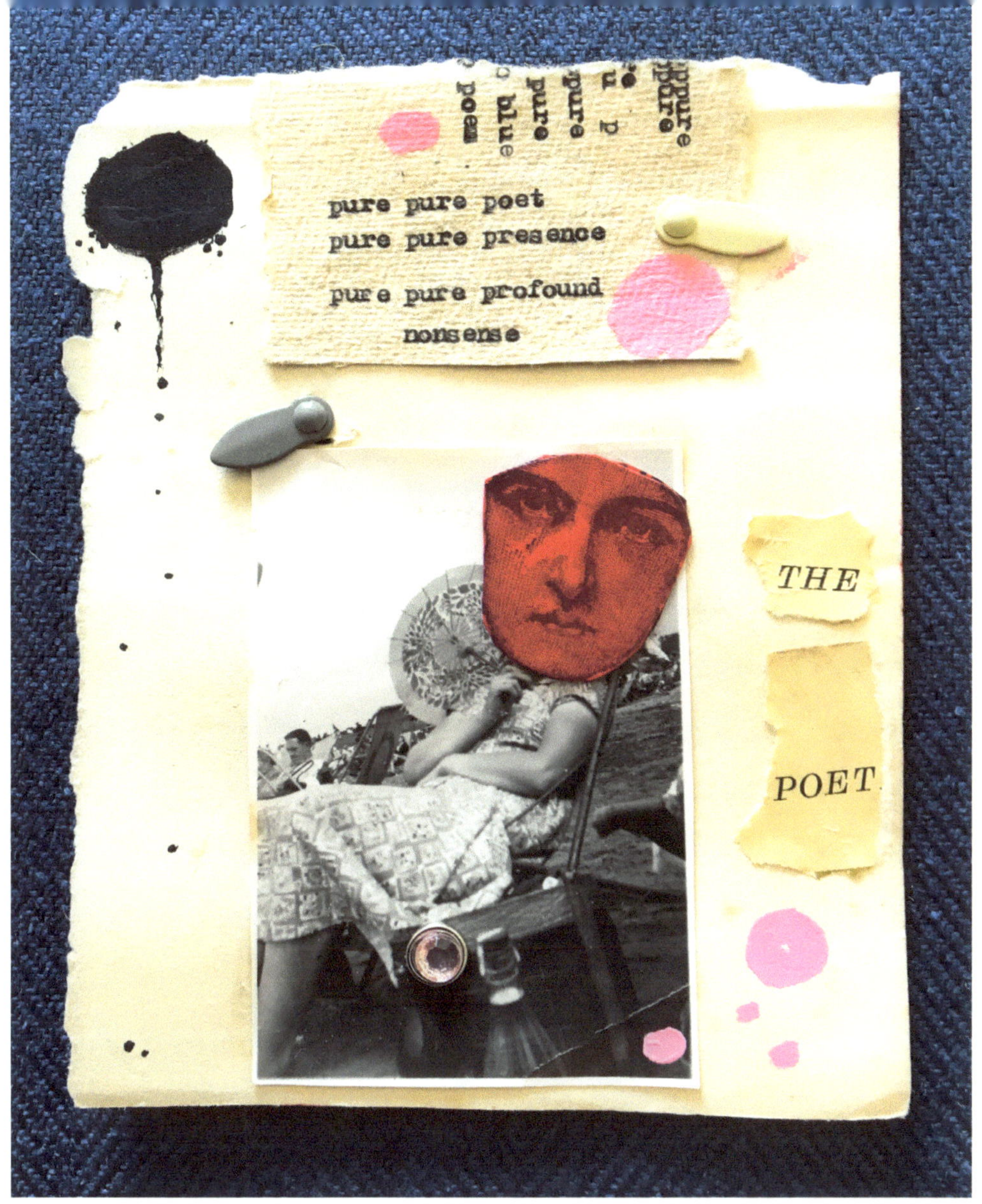
pure pure poet
pure pure presence
pure pure profound
nonsense
THE
POET

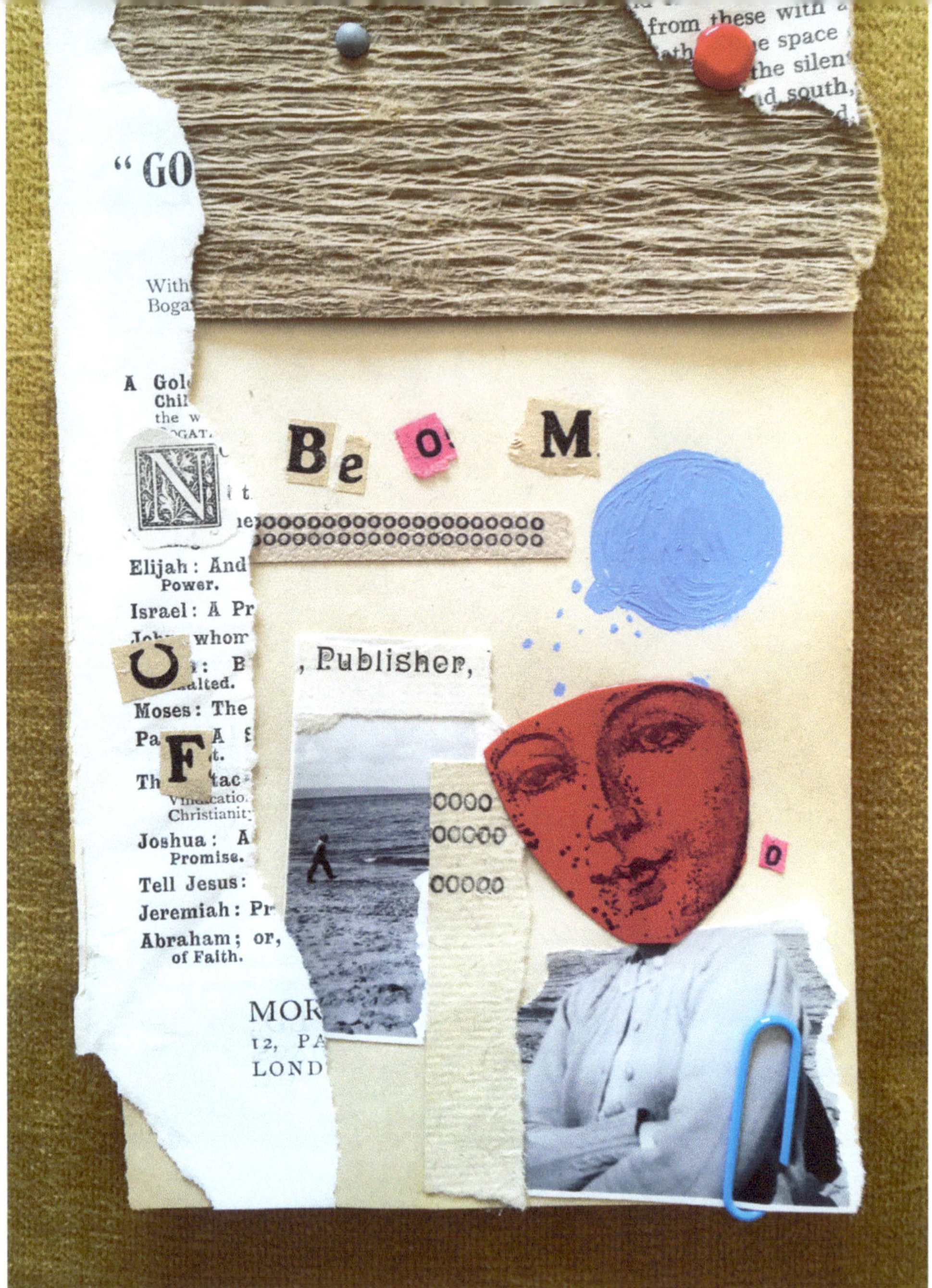
from these with a
e space
the silen
d south,
“GO
With
Boga
A Gol
Chil
the w
Be
M
Elijah: And
Power.
Israel: A Pr
whom
alted.
Moses: The
F
Christianit
Joshua: A
Promise.
Tell Jesus:
Jeremiah: Pr
Abraham; or,
of Faith.
, Publisher,
MOR
12, PA
LOND

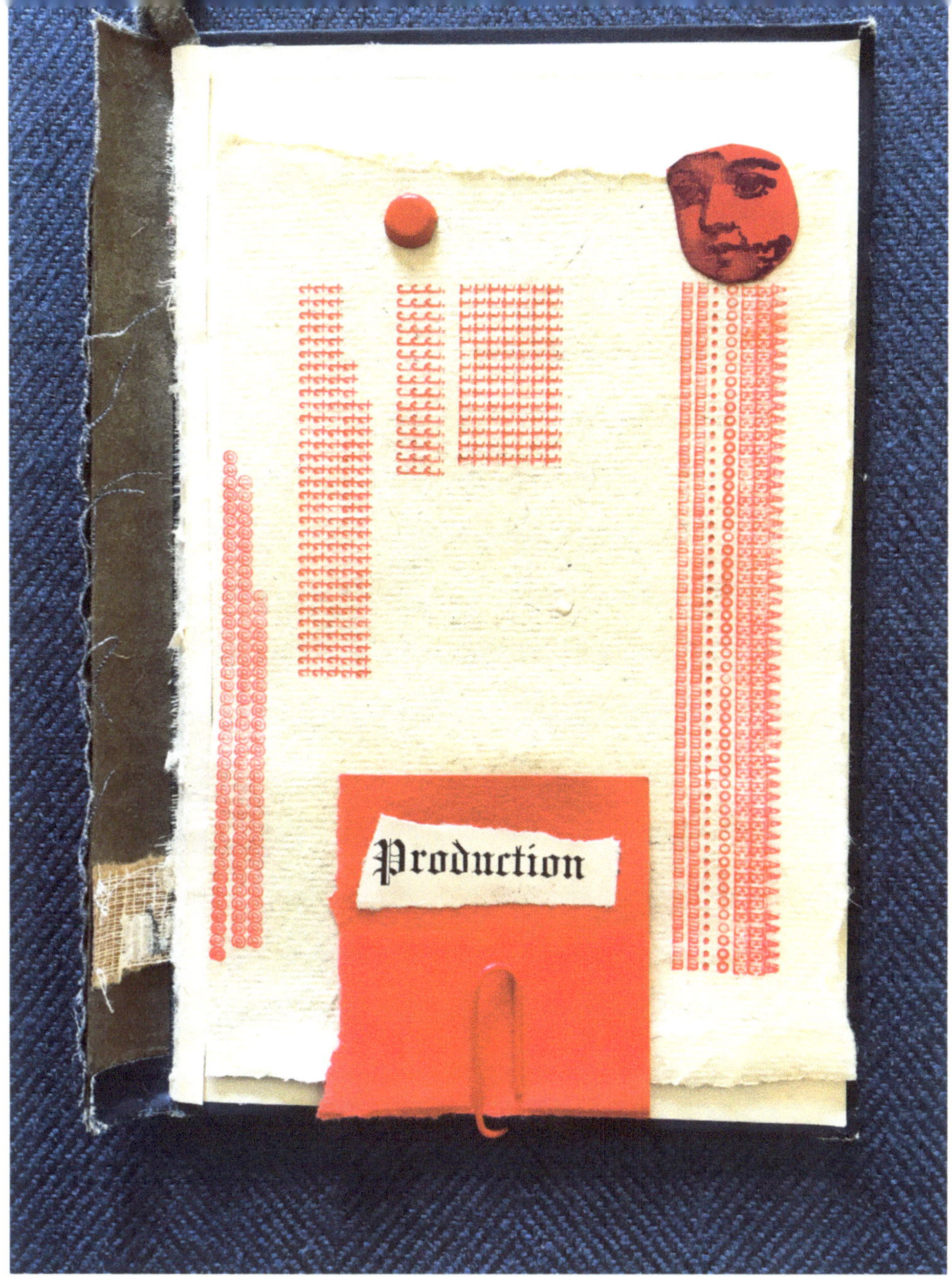
Production

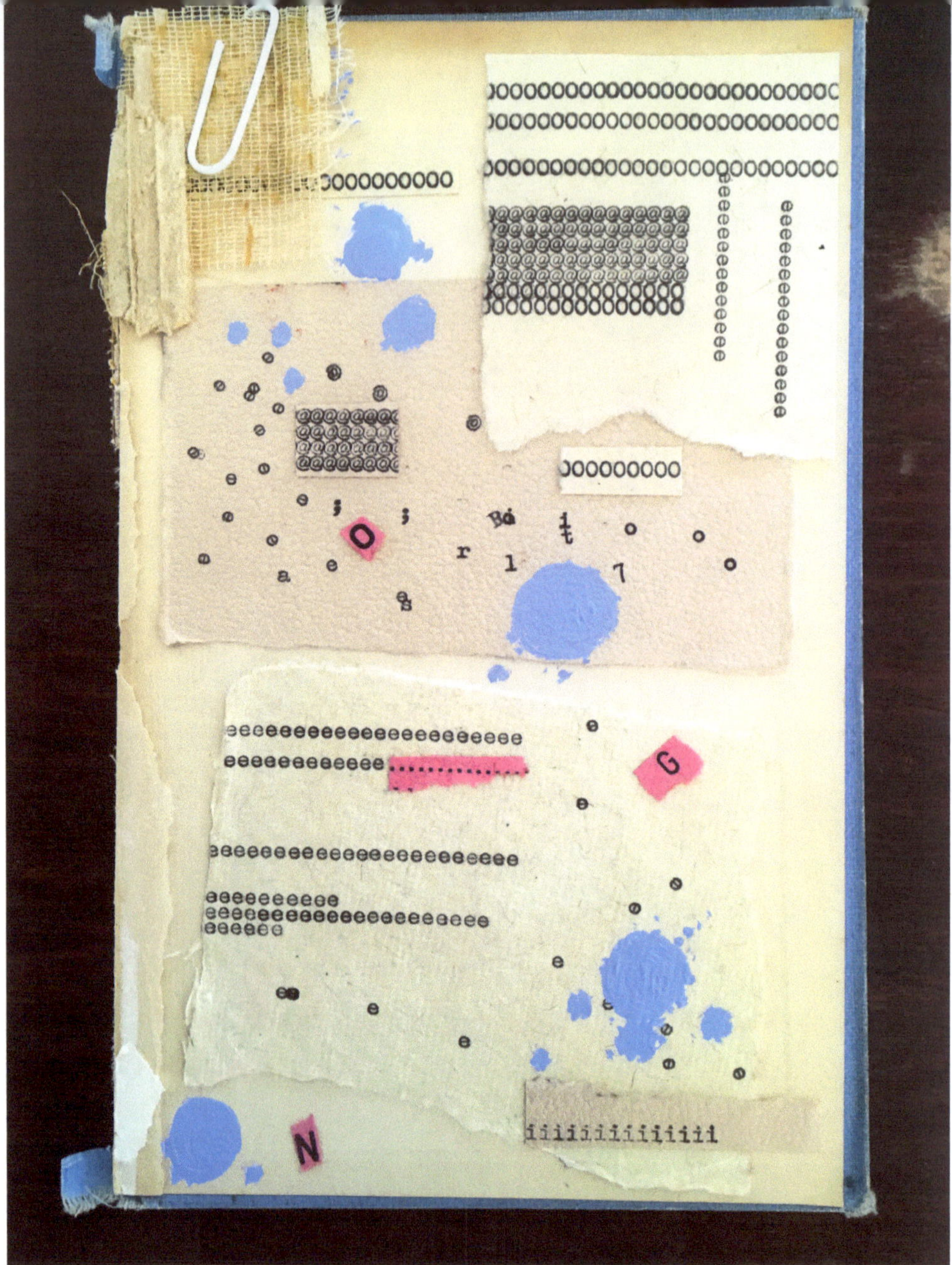

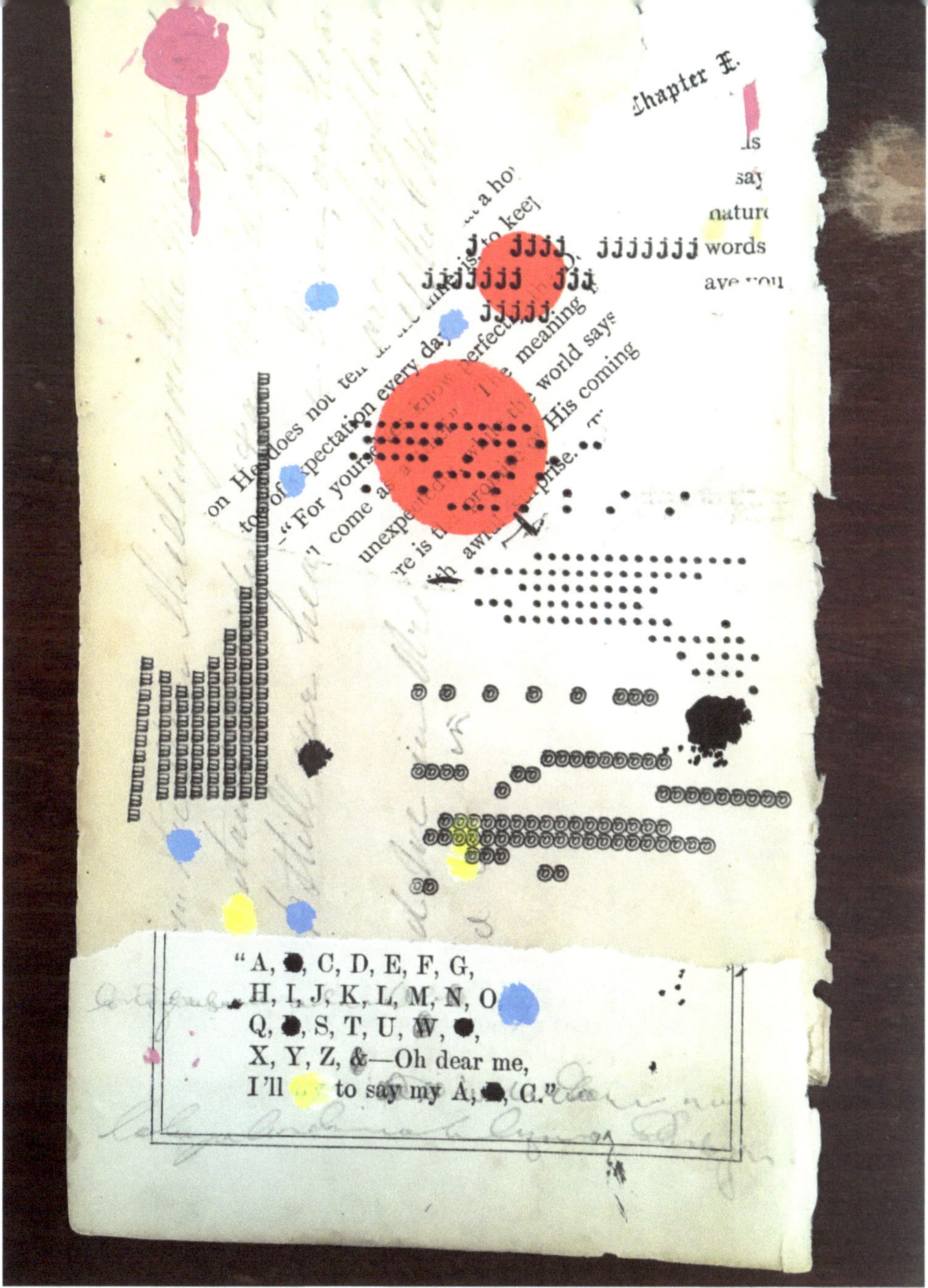
Chapter X.
"A, ●, C, D, E, F, G,
H, I, J, K, L, M, N, O
Q, ●, S, T, U, W, ●,
X, Y, Z, &—Oh dear me,
I'll to say my A, ●, C."

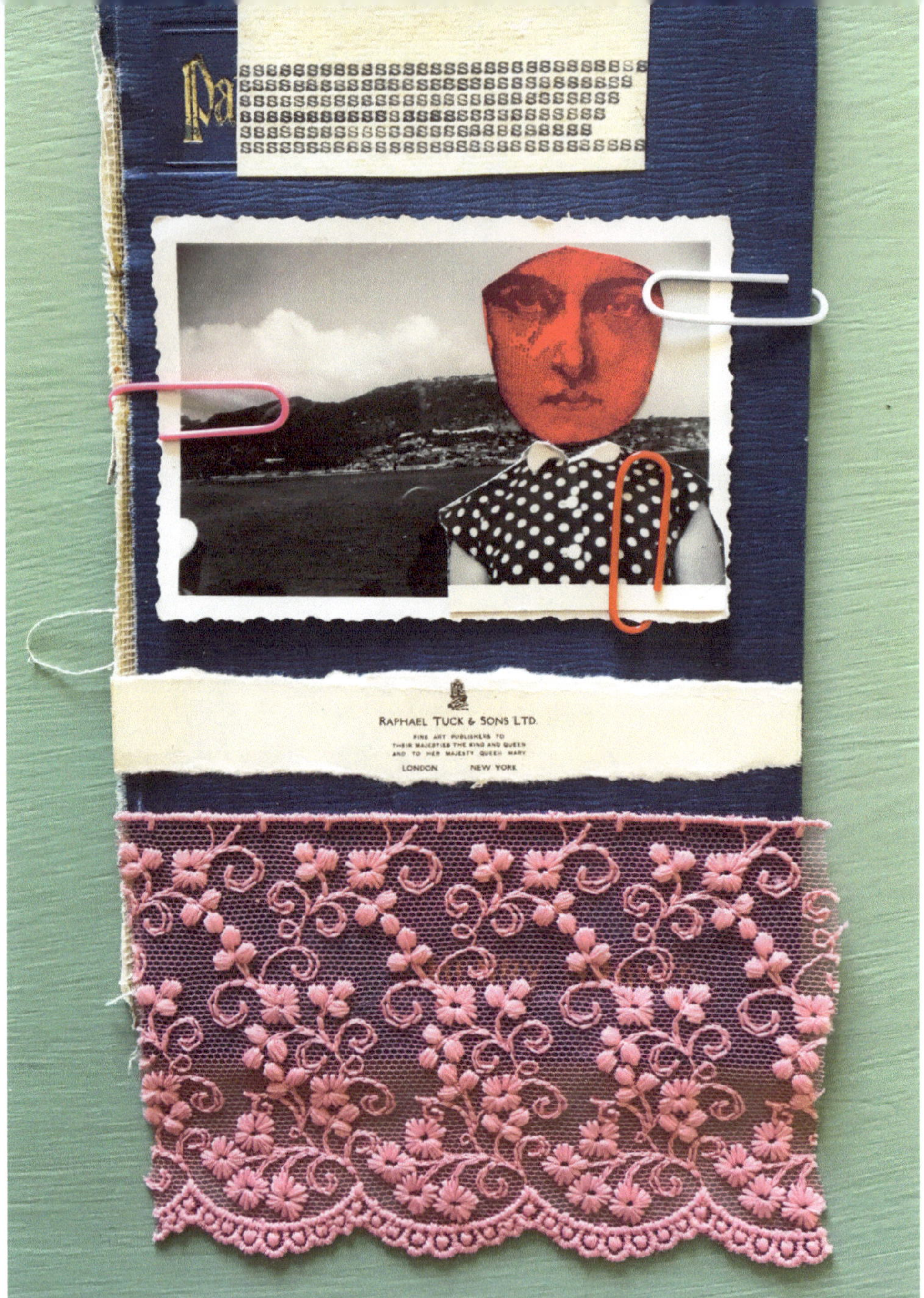
RAPHAEL TUCK & SONS LTD.
FINE ART PUBLISHERS TO
THEIR MAJESTIES THE KING AND QUEEN
AND TO HER MAJESTY QUEEN MARY
LONDON NEW YORK

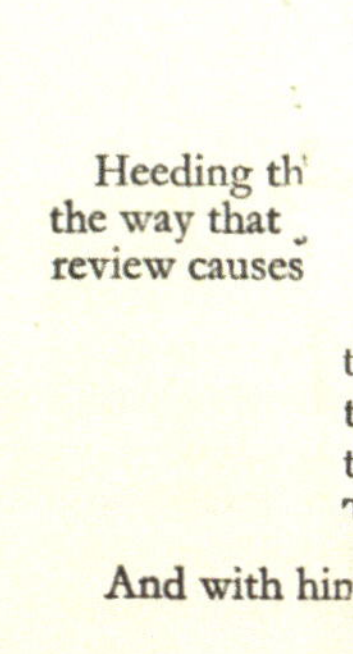
Heeding th
the way that
review causes
throttle. See: carburetor
tie rod. See: steering mechan
tires. See: wheels & tires
And with hin

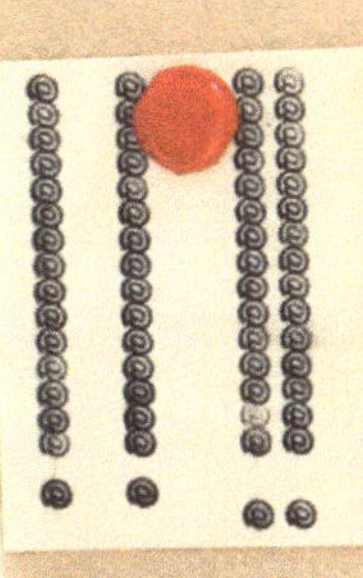
PATER

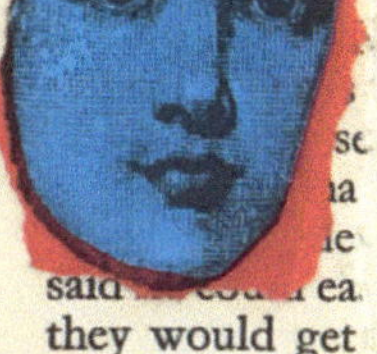
THE only
earlier time
larly attrac
and was especia
covered in allia
detected, in fact
very act, he was
in truth, had le
duced to the l
of his ingratitu
each and all of h
of course, Adam
they would get
The hearth,
its spirit
the price i
the arm is
and all is

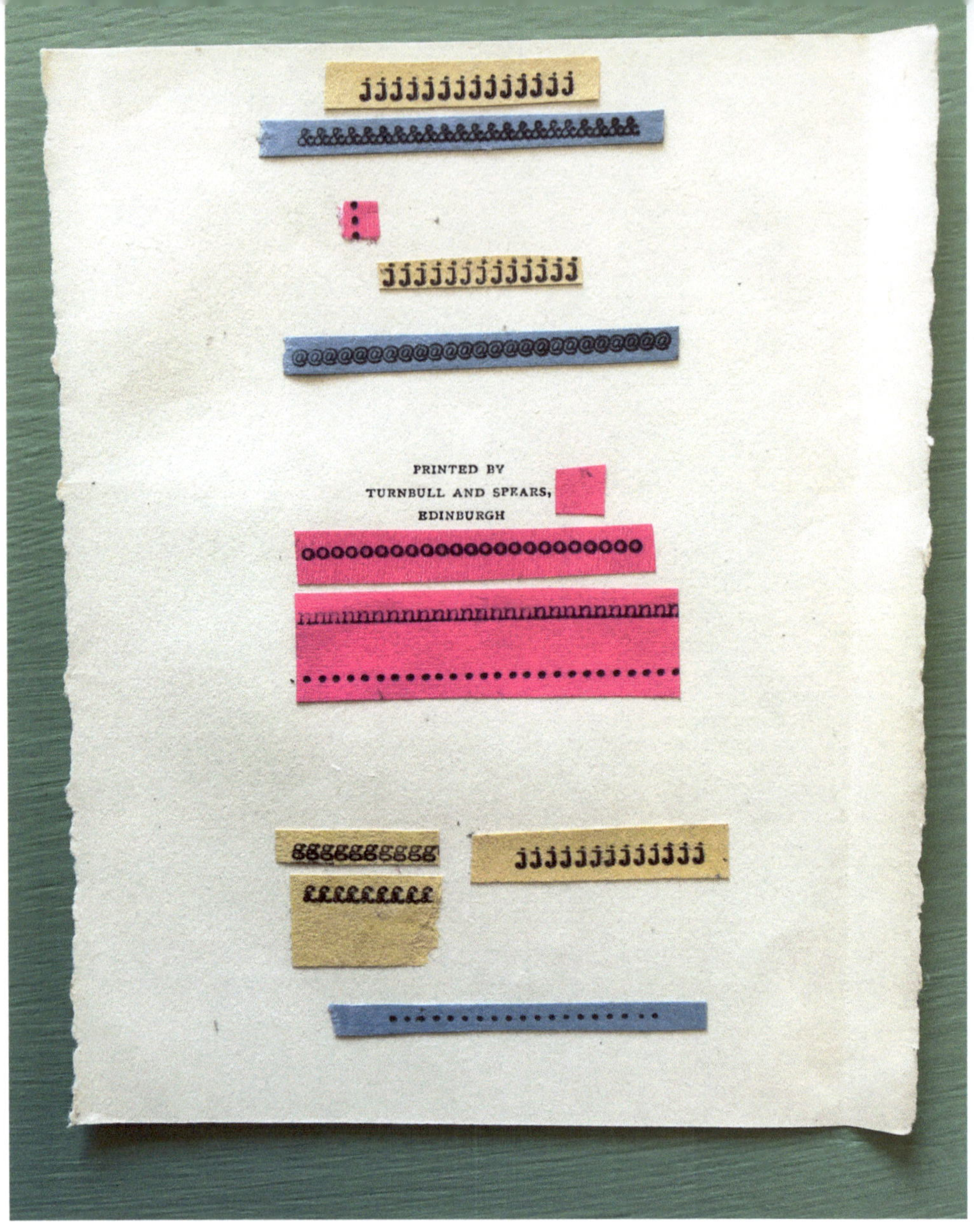
PRINTED BY
TURNBULL AND SPEARS,
EDINBURGH

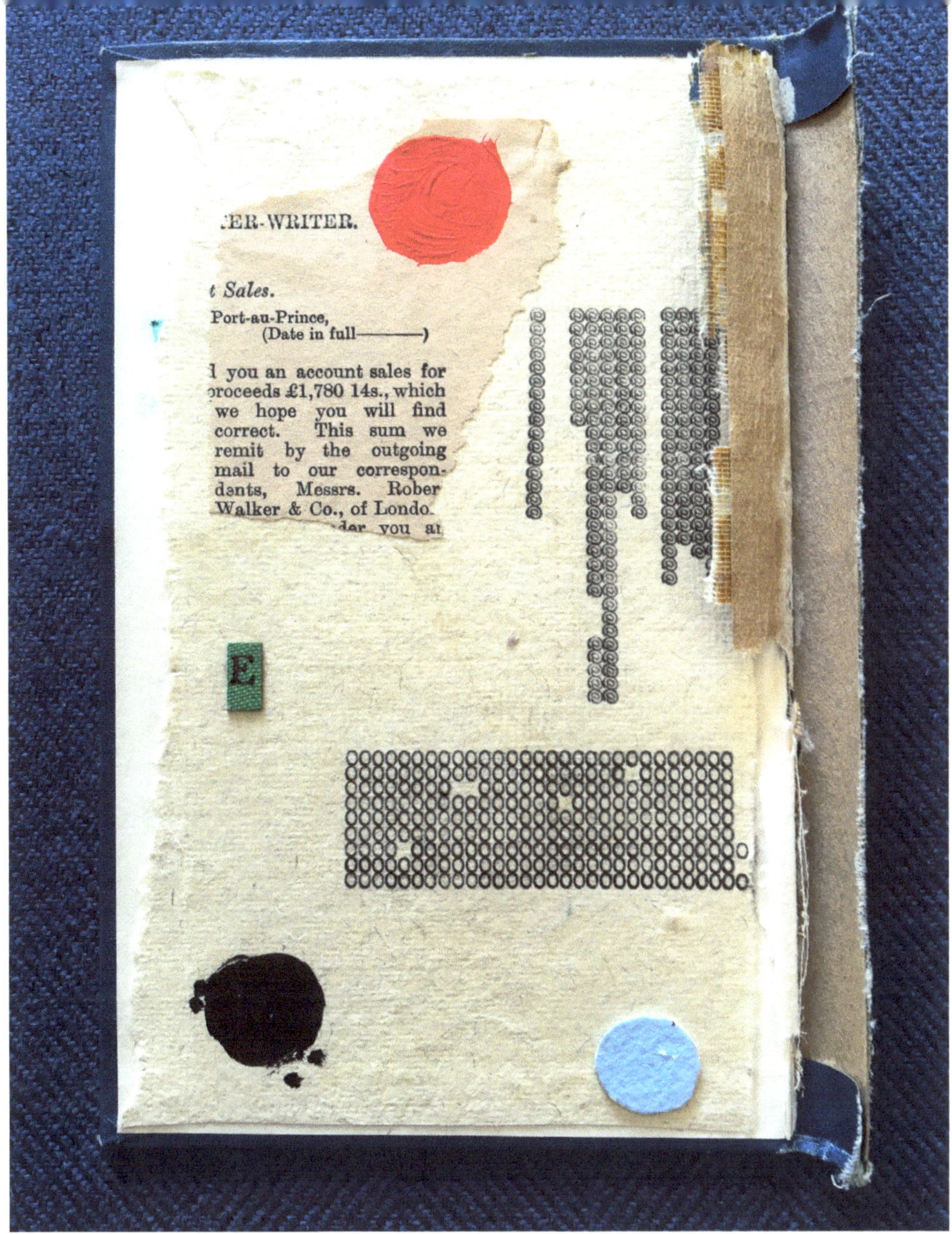
ER-WRITER.
Sales.
Port-au-Prince,
(Date in full———)
you an account sales for
roceeds £1,780 14s., which
we hope you will find
correct. This sum we
remit by the outgoing
mail to our correspon-
dents, Messrs. Rober
Walker & Co., of Londo
E

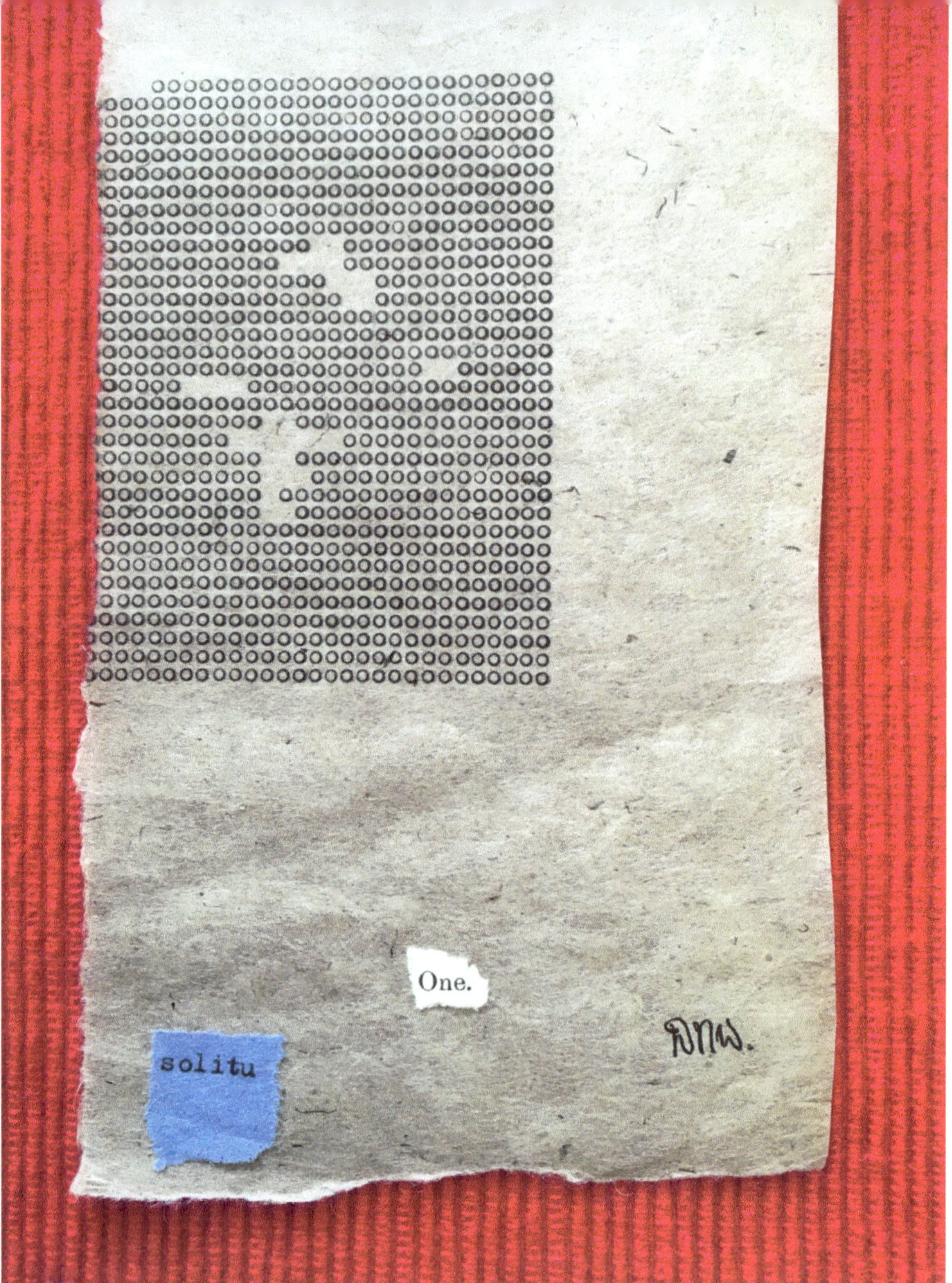
One.
solitu

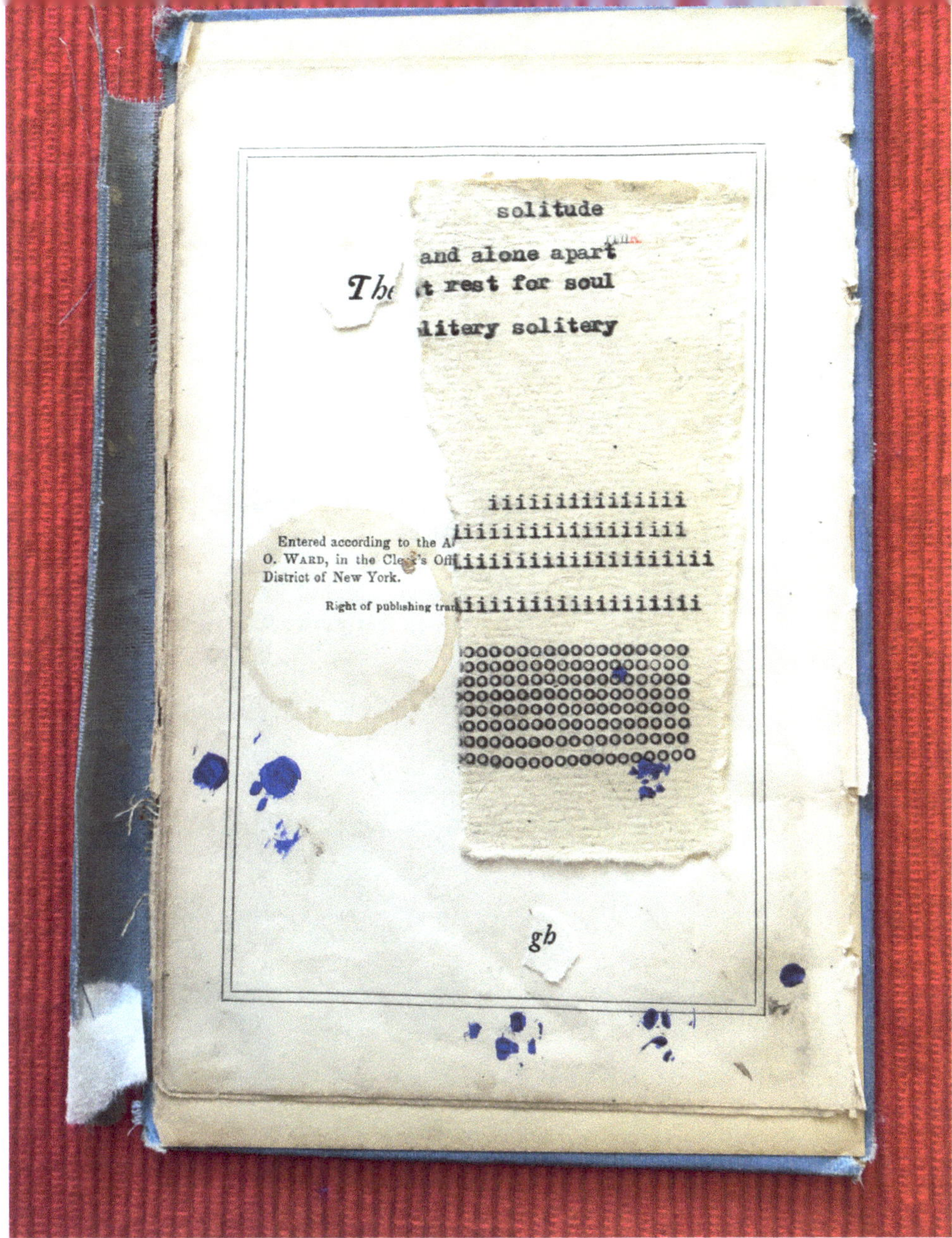
solitude
and alone apart
The
t rest for soul
litery solitery
Entered according to the A
O. WARD, in the Cle 's Off
District of New York.
Right of publishing tra
gb

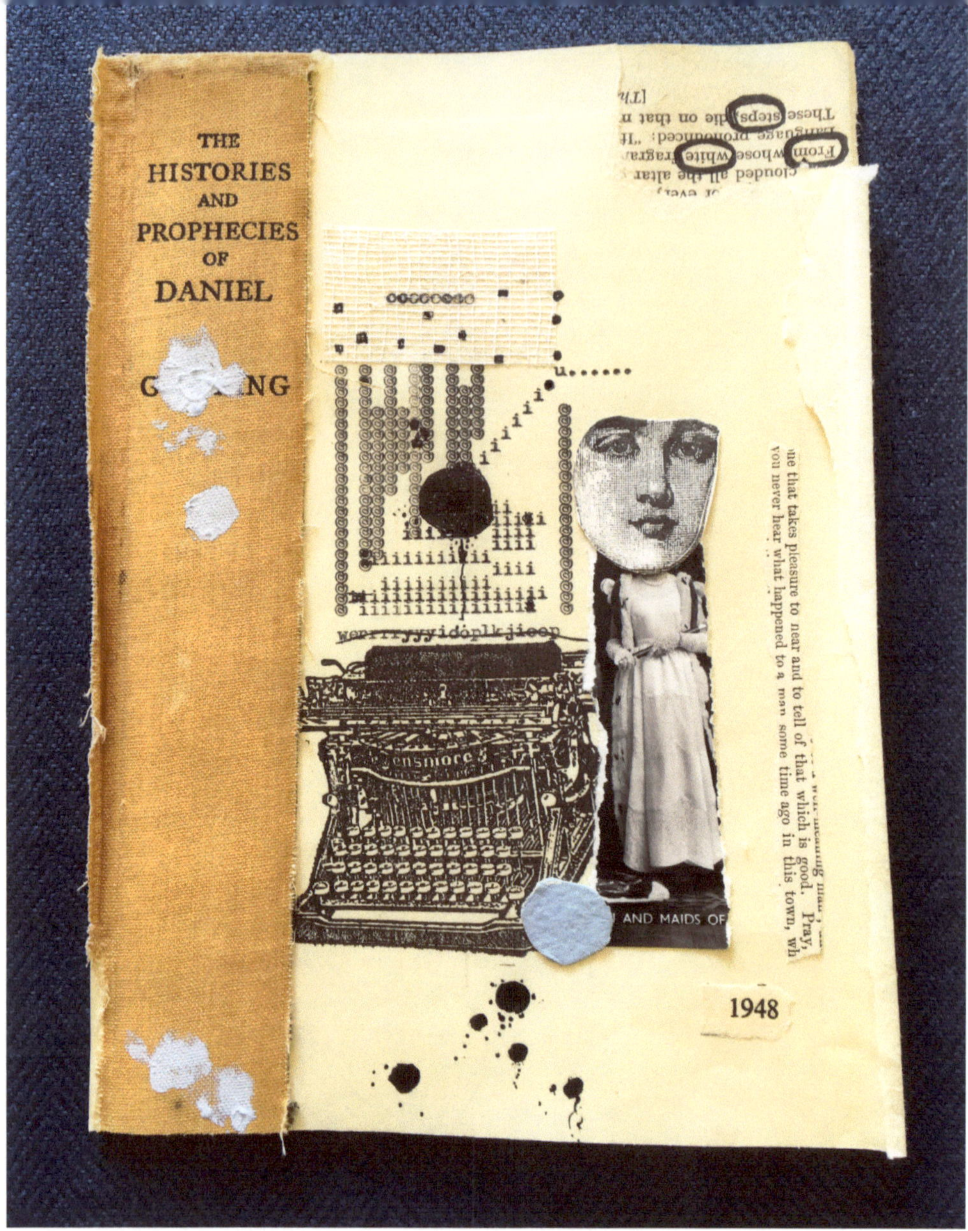
THE
HISTORIES
AND
PROPHECIES
OF
DANIEL
he that takes pleasure to hear and to tell of that which is good. Pray,
you never hear what happened to a man some time ago in this town, wh
AND MAIDS OF
1948

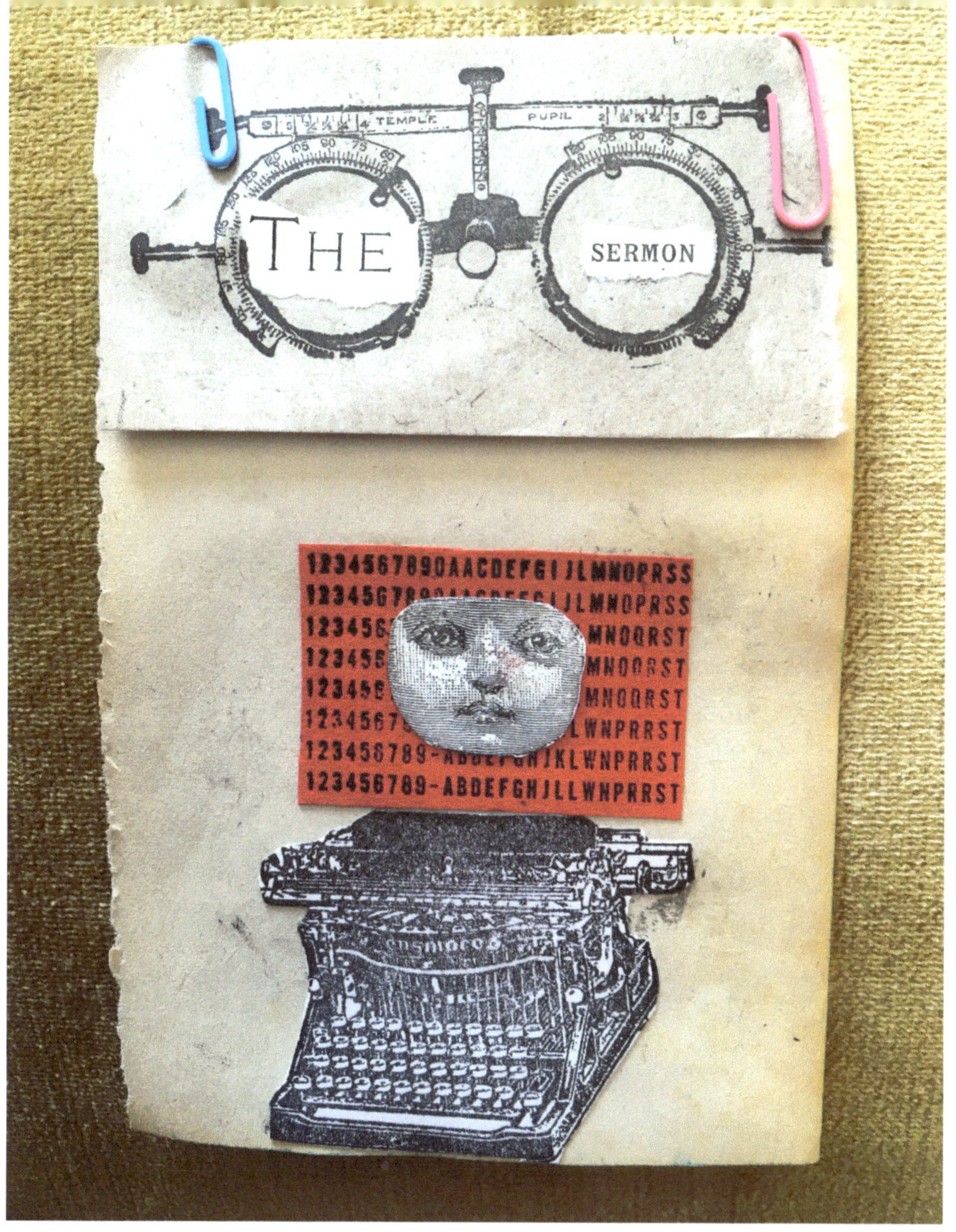
TEMPLE
PUPIL
THE
SERMON
1234567890AACDEFGIJLMNOPRSS
123456789-ABDEFGHJLLWNPRRST

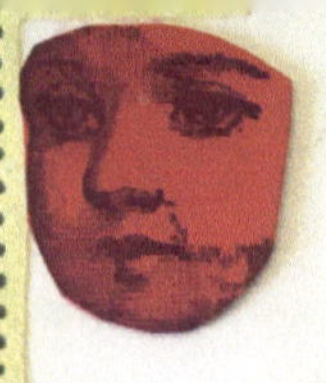

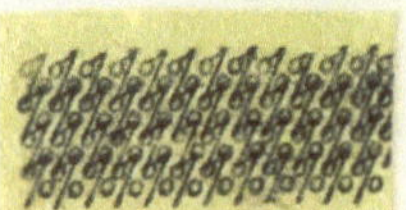

The Liberty of Sonship.

B

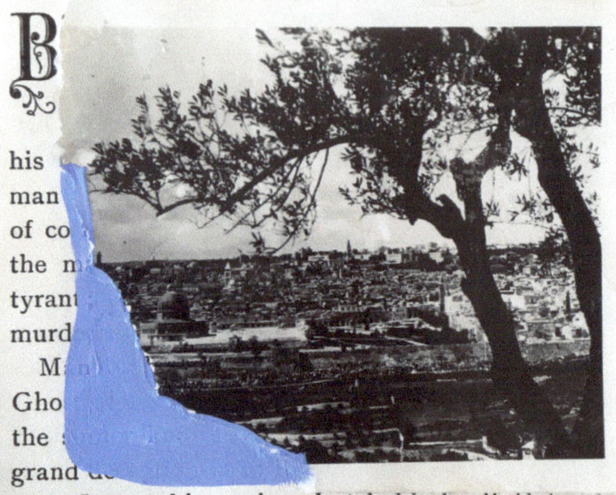

his
man
of co
the m
tyrant
murd
Ma
Gho
the
grand
This flatters his vanity; but behind self, Satan is
ever b reigns,
perha ill and
depra
In ord Son of God
has come, der law, to
redeem from the bondage of Satan, to save from
the power o deliver from the fear of
death. Chr to destroy (λυση, unloose
or untie) the works of the devil, which, in man,

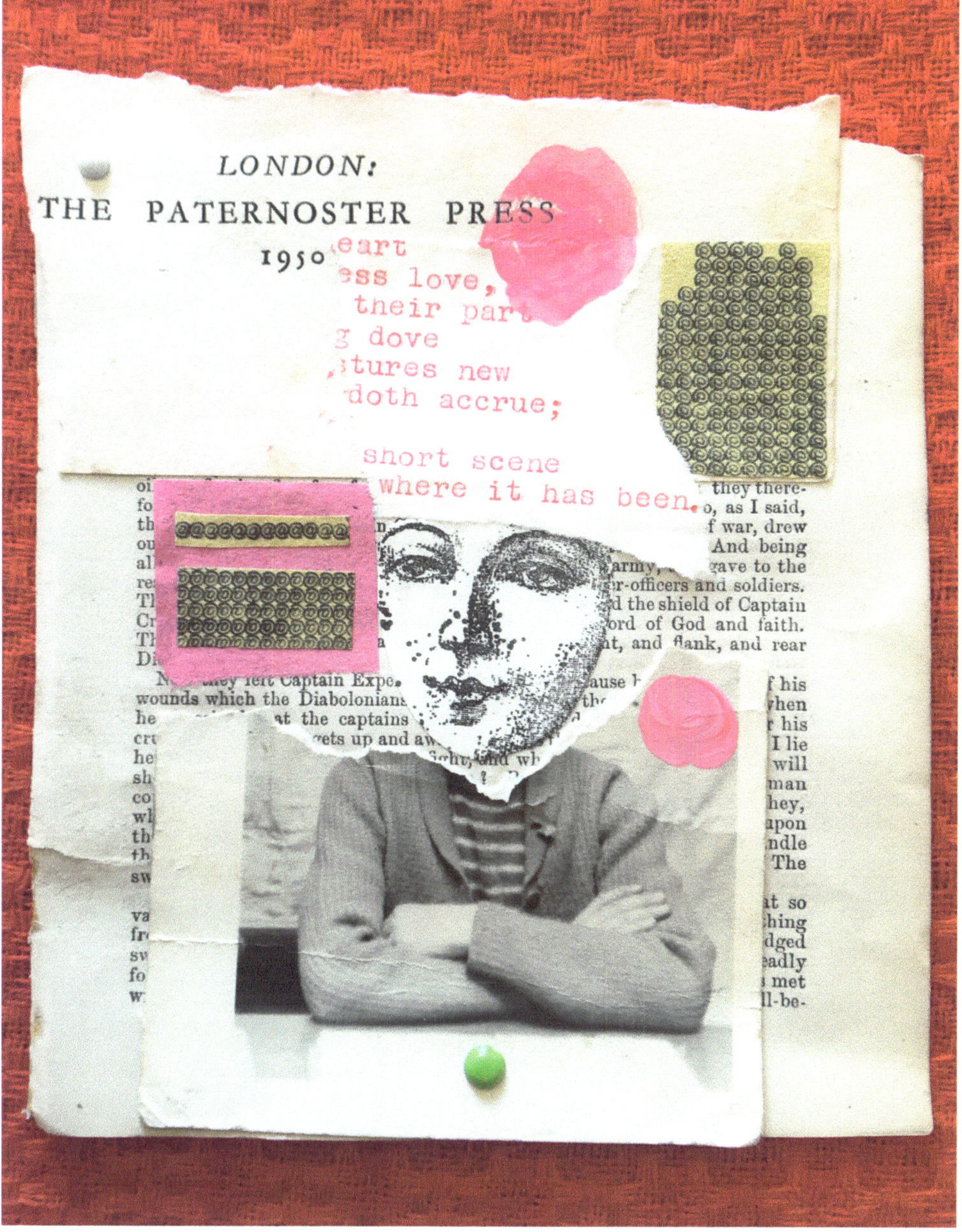
LONDON:
THE PATERNOSTER PRESS
1950
eart
ess love,
their part
g dove
tures new
doth accrue;
short scene
where it has been.

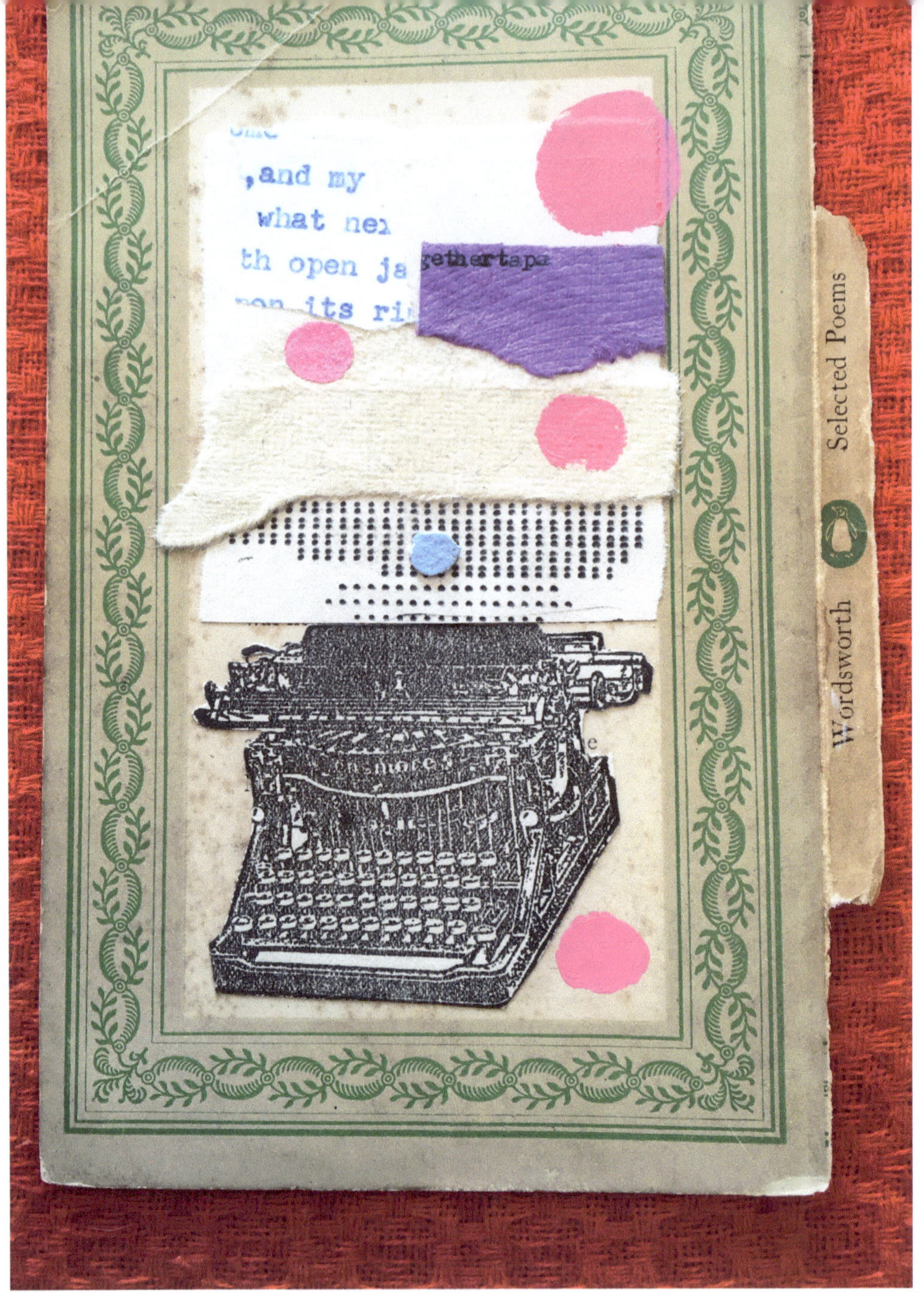
,and my
what nex
th open ja
gethertapa
Selected Poems
Wordsworth

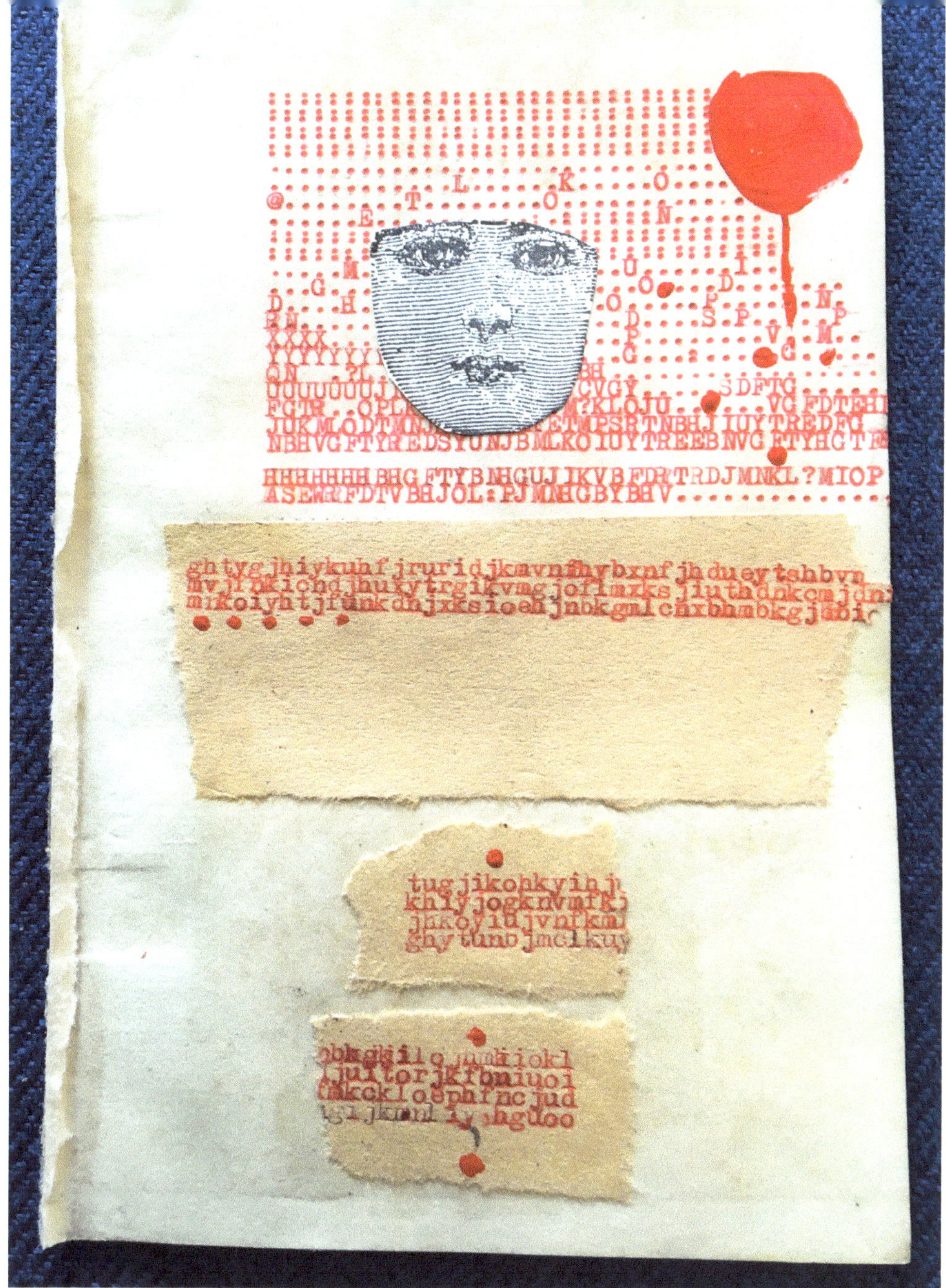

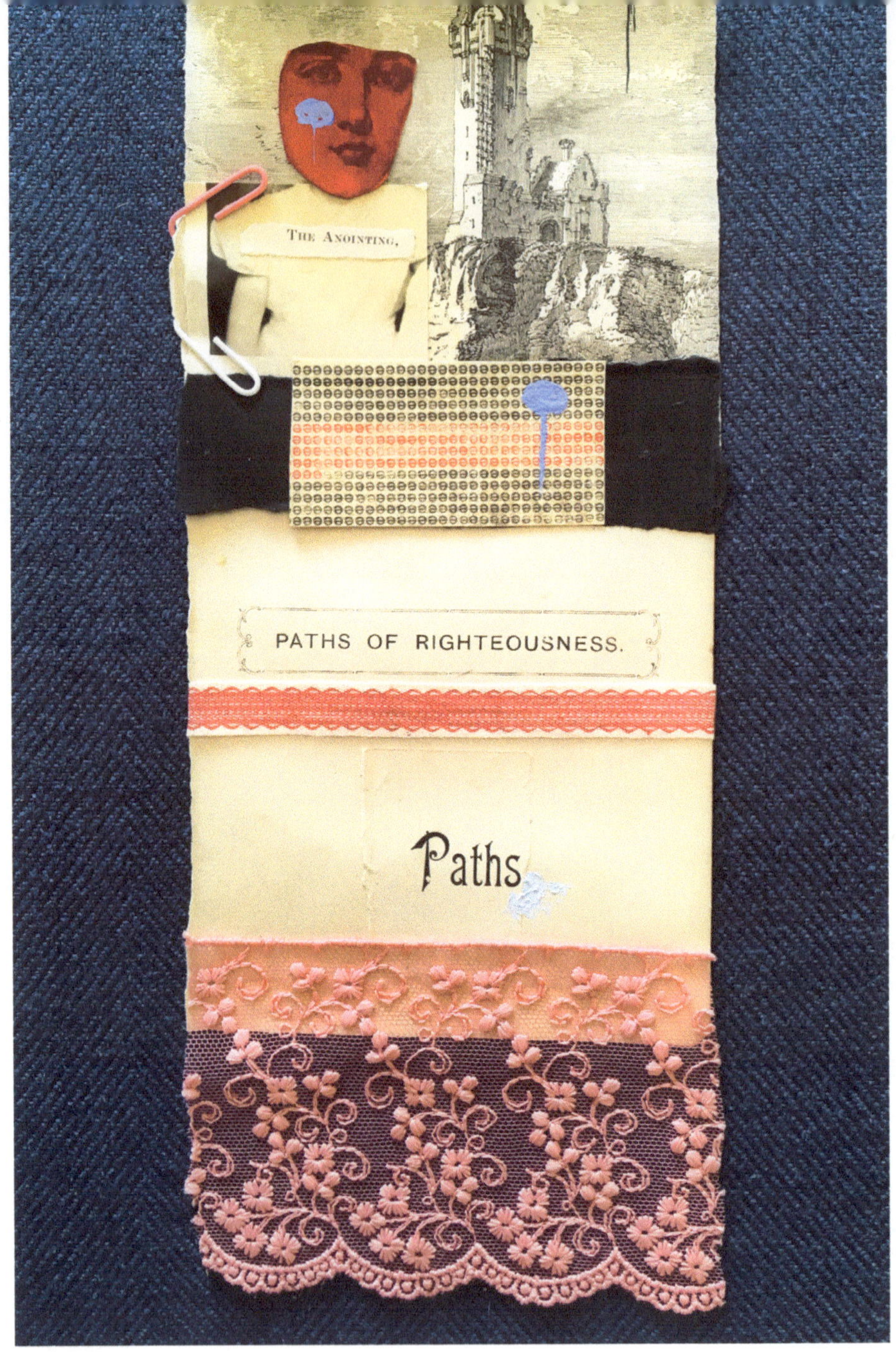
The Anointing.
PATHS OF RIGHTEOUSNESS.
Paths

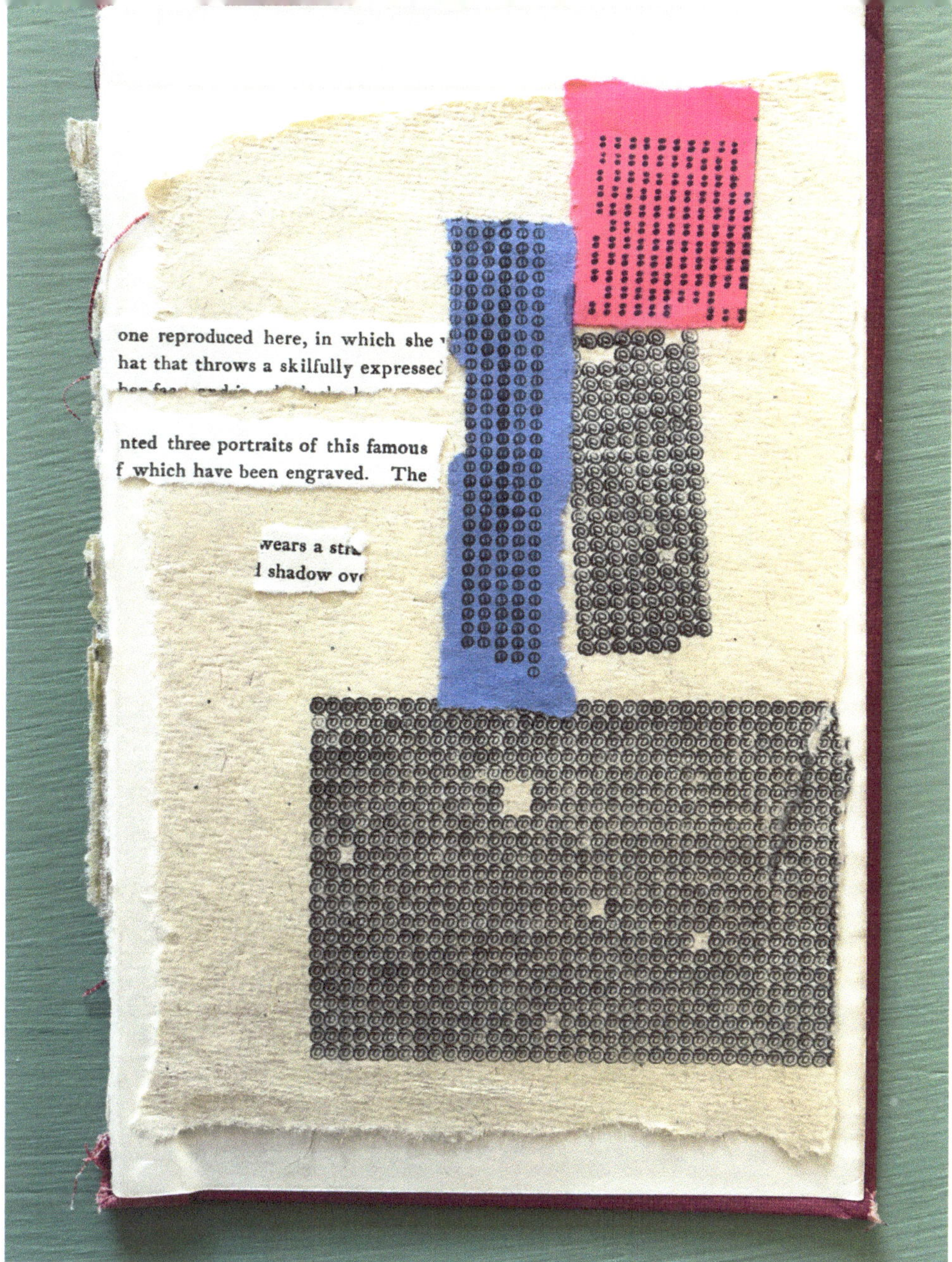
one reproduced here, in which she
hat that throws a skilfully expressed
nted three portraits of this famous
f which have been engraved. The
wears a str
shadow ov

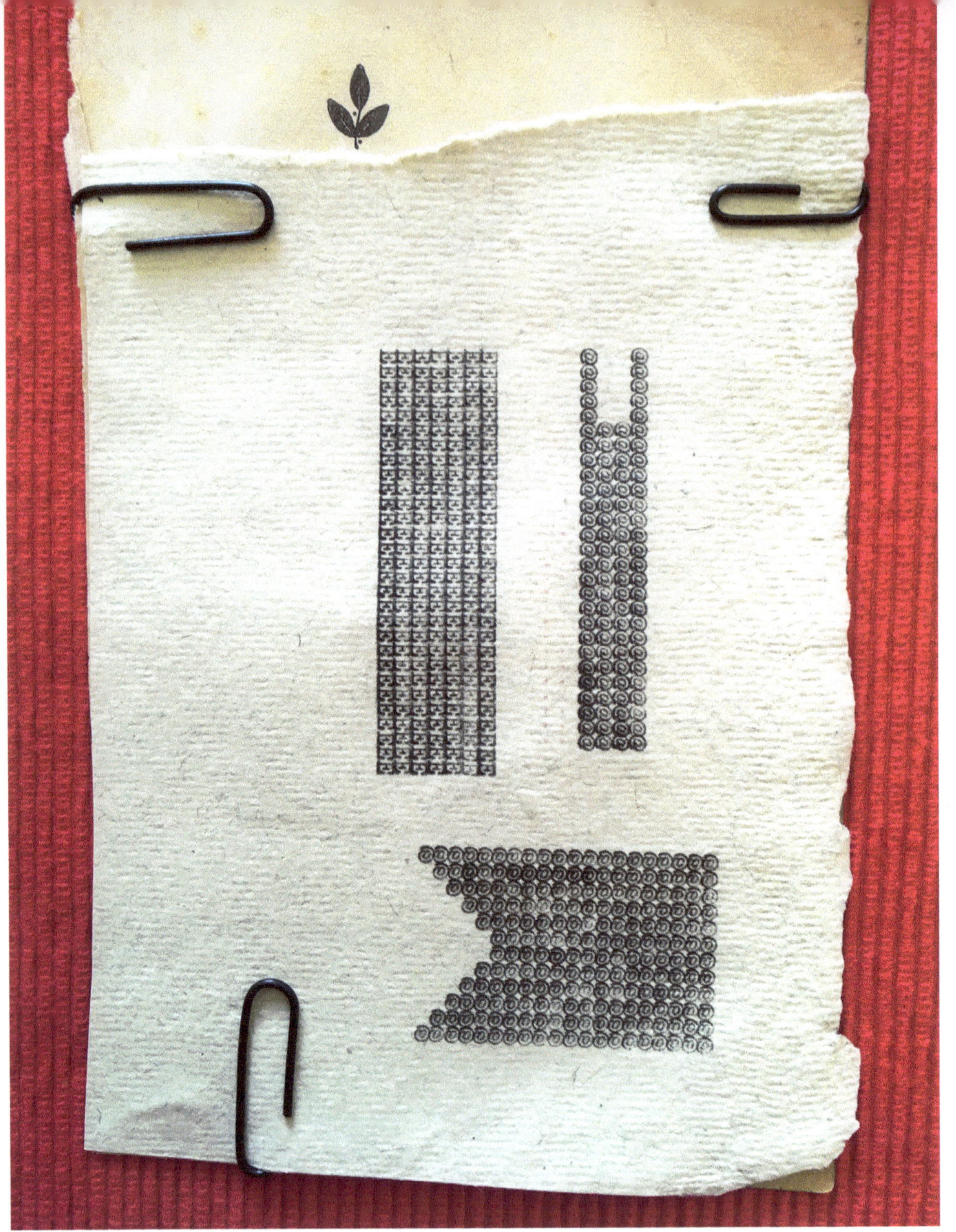

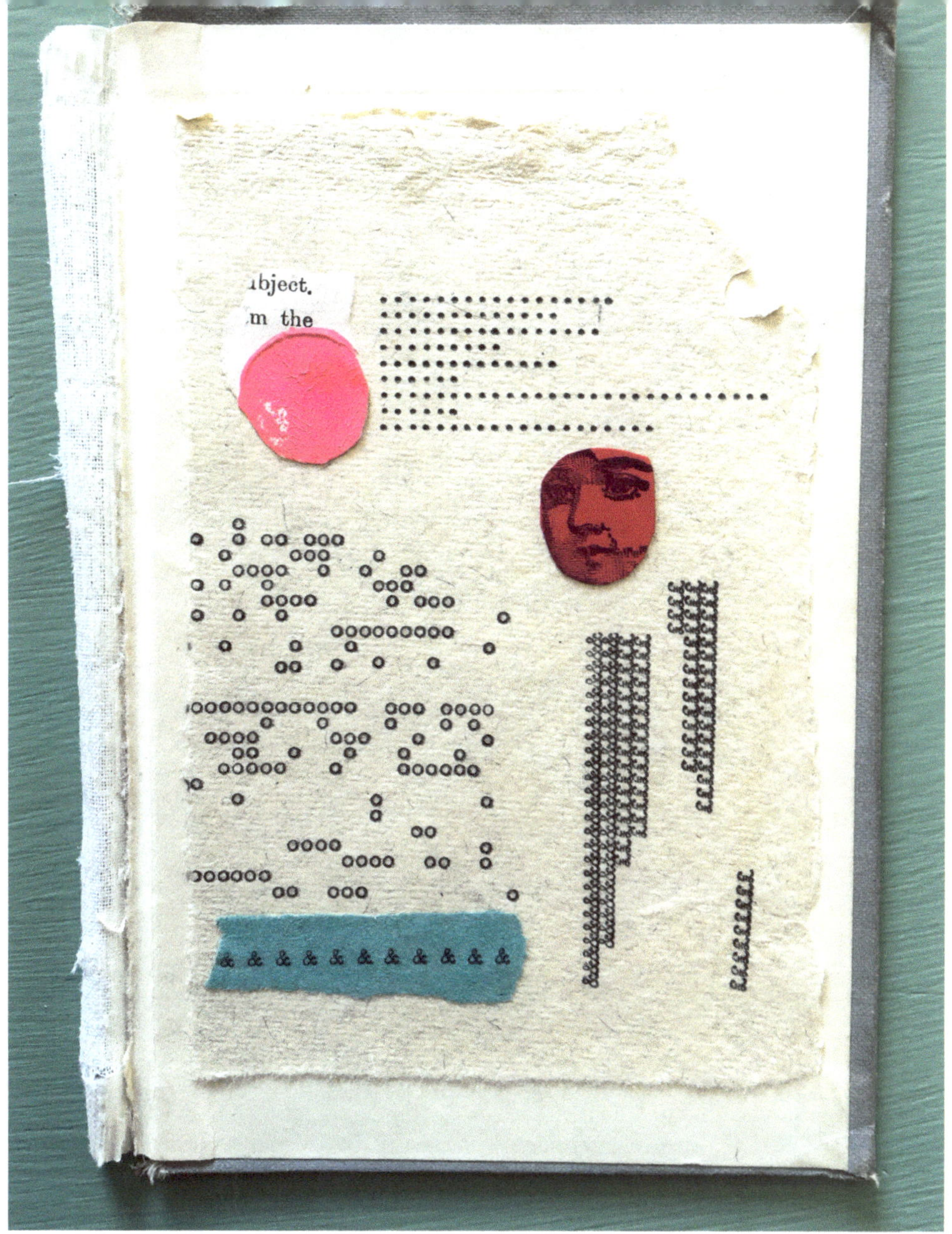
bject.
m the

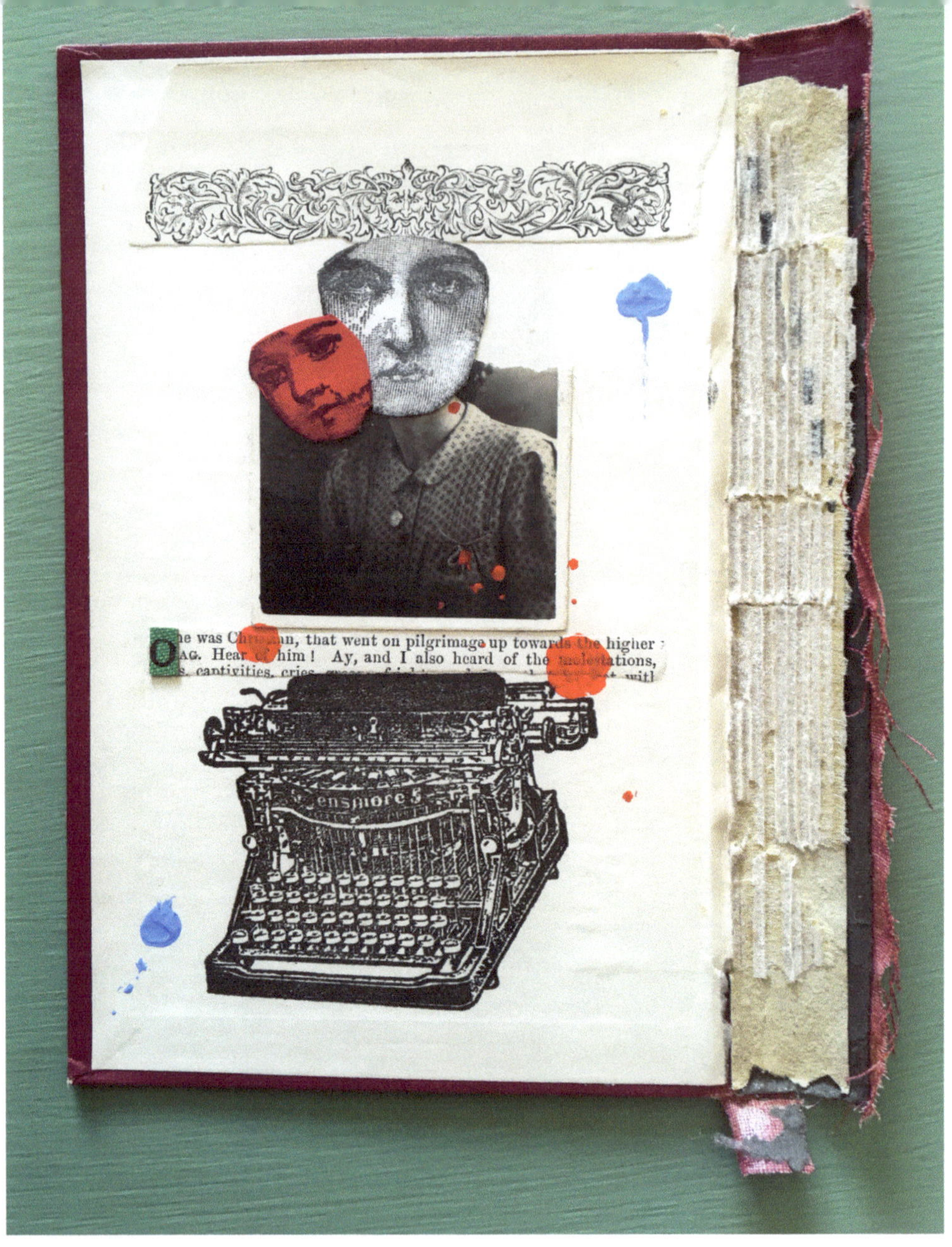
O
he was Ch an, that went on pilgrimage up towards higher
AG. Hear him! Ay, and I also heard of the ations,
s. captivities, cries

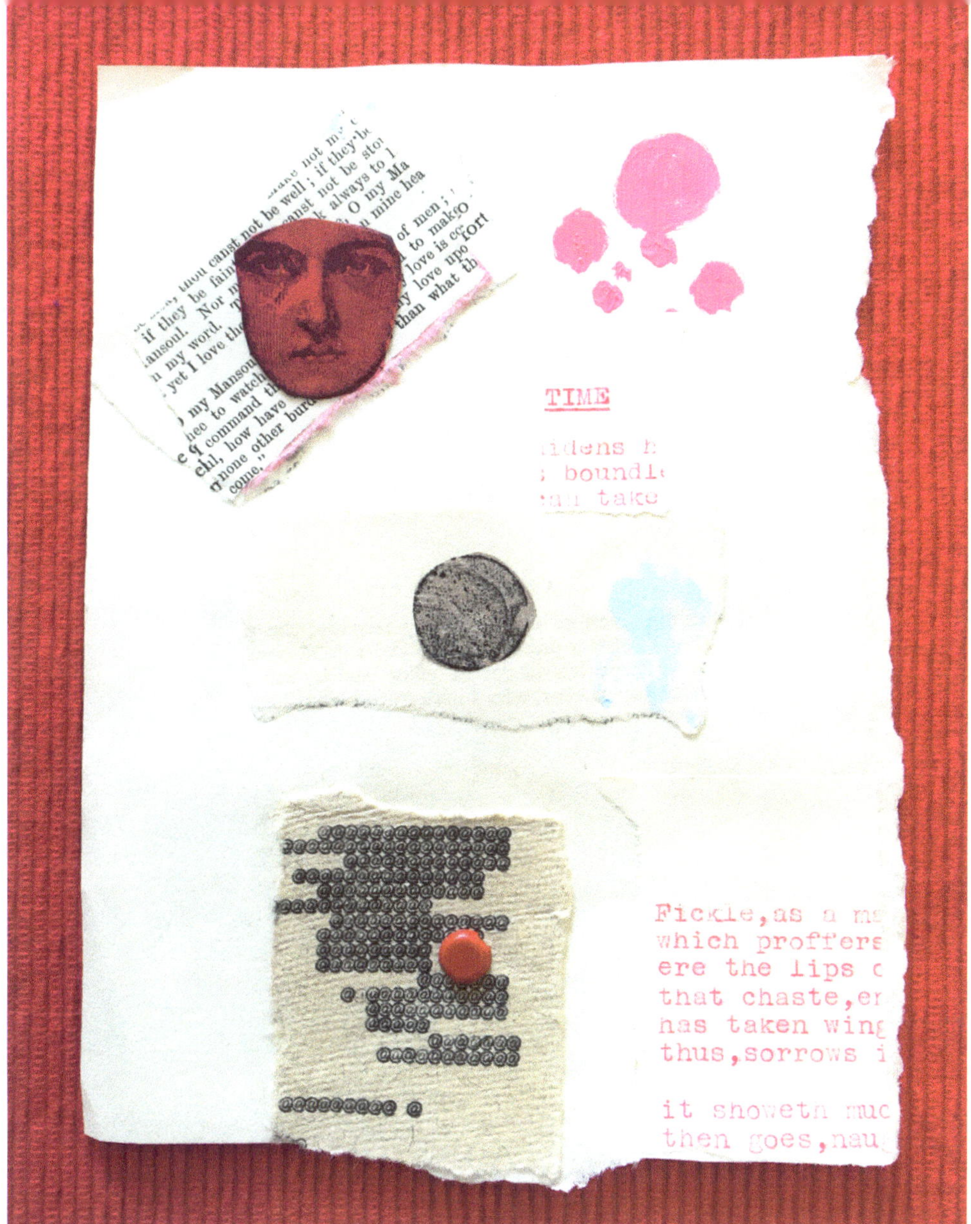
TIME
Fickle,as a m
which proffers
ere the lips
that chaste,e
has taken win
thus,sorrows
it showeth muc
then goes,nau

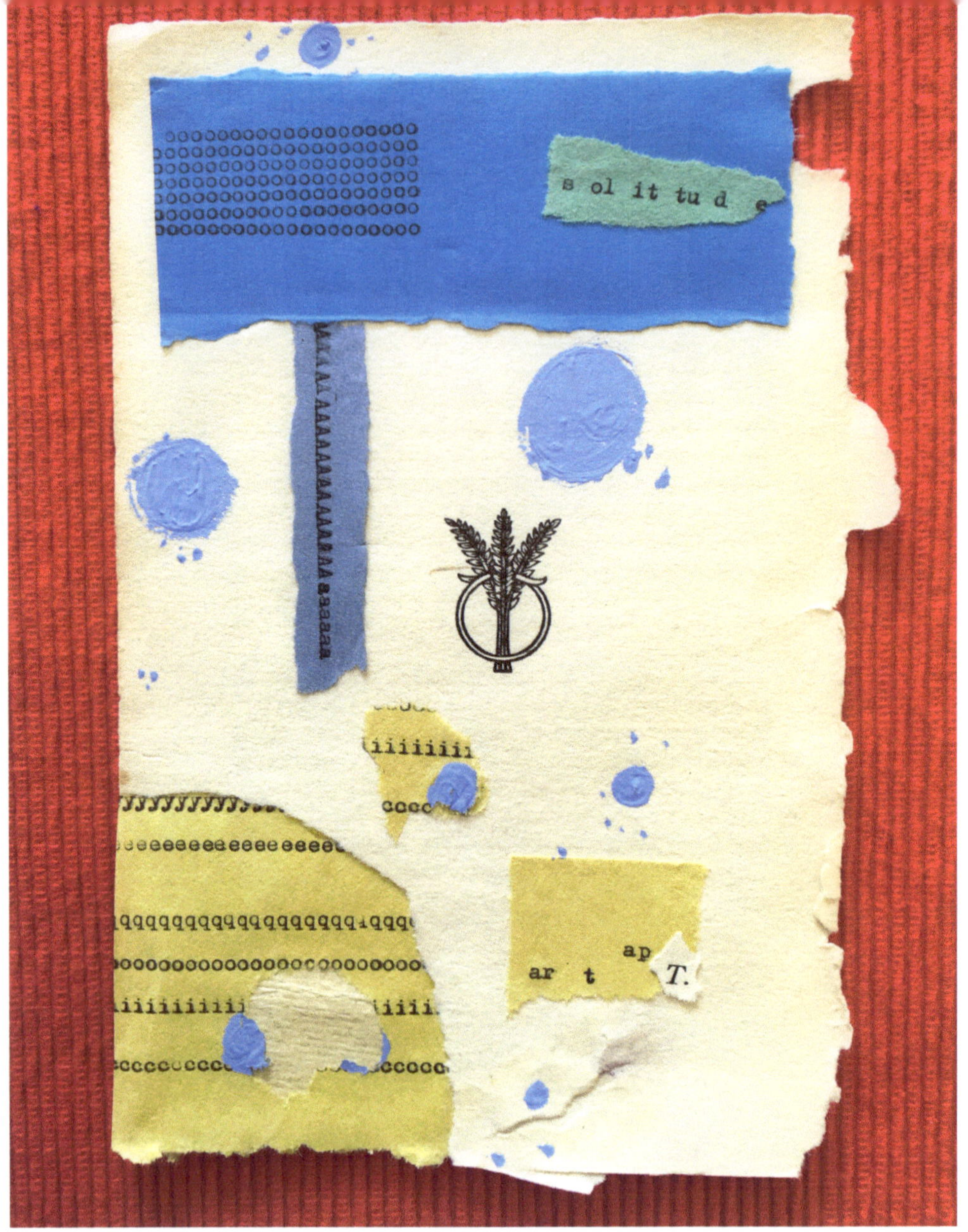
s ol it tu d e
ap
ar t T.

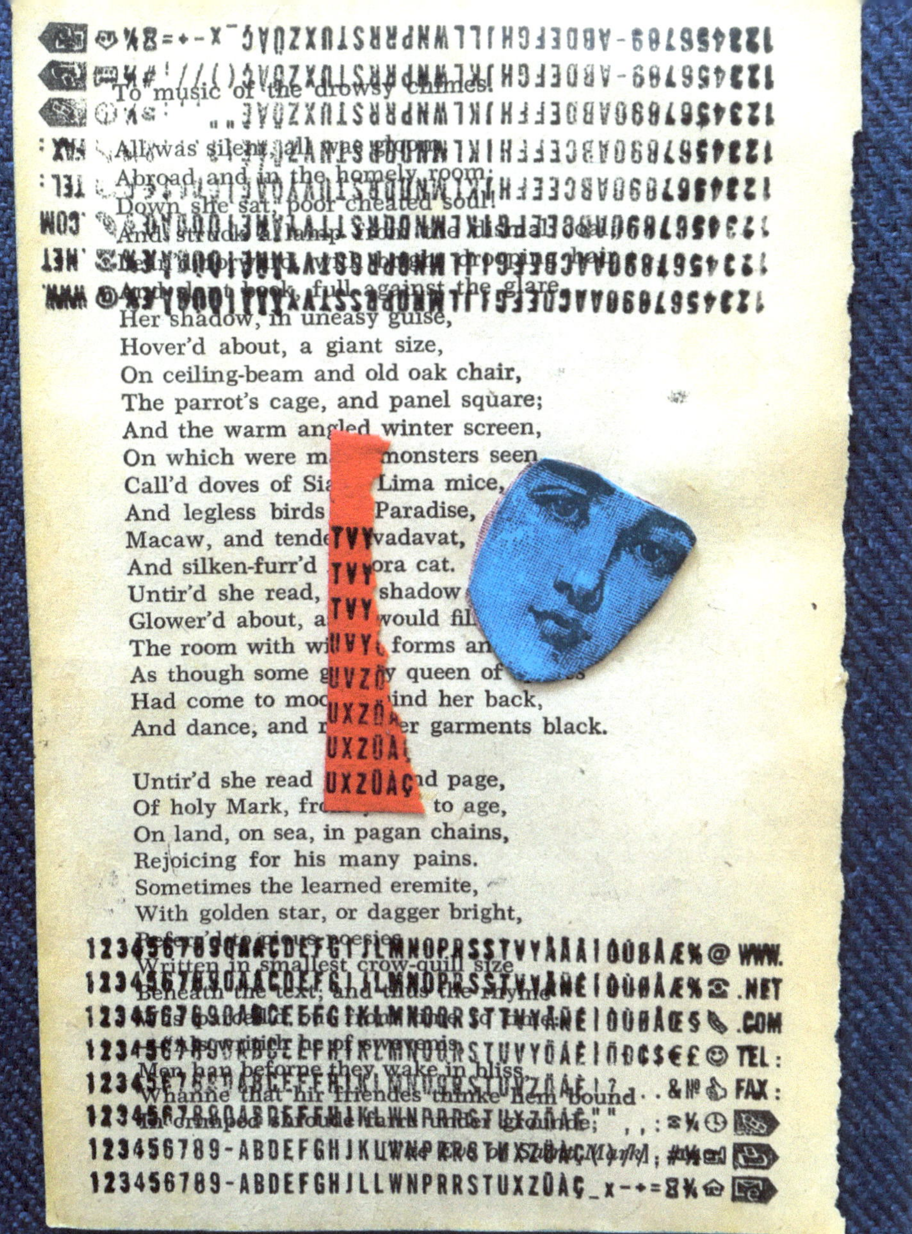
To music of the drowsy chimes!
Abroad, and in the homely room;
Down she sat, poor cheated soul!
And back, full against the glare.
Her shadow, in uneasy guise,
Hover'd about, a giant size,
On ceiling-beam and old oak chair,
The parrot's cage, and panel square;
And the warm angled winter screen,
On which were m monsters seen
Call'd doves of Sia Lima mice,
And legless birds Paradise,
Macaw, and tende vadavat,
And silken-furr'd ora cat.
Untir'd she read, shadow
Glower'd about, a would fil
The room with wi forms an
As though some g y queen of
Had come to moc ind her back,
And dance, and r er garments black.
Untir'd she read d page,
Of holy Mark, fr to age,
On land, on sea, in pagan chains,
Rejoicing for his many pains.
Sometimes the learned eremite,
With golden star, or dagger bright,
Written in smallest crow-quill size
Beneath the text; and thus the rhyme
Men han beforne they wake in bliss,
Whanne that hir friendes thinke hem bound
123456789-ABDEFGHJLLWNPRRSTUXZÜAÇ_x-+=8%

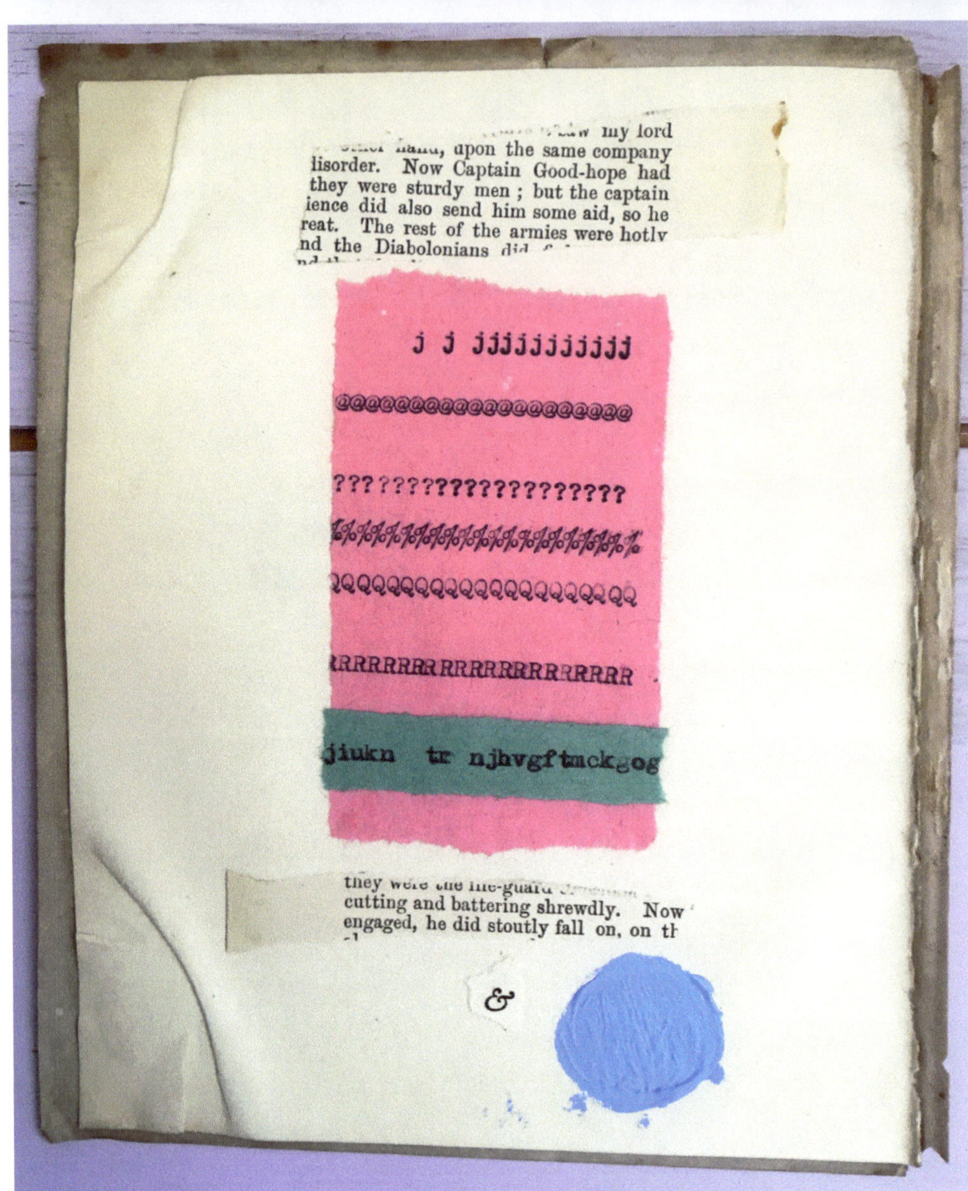
my lord
upon the same company
lisorder. Now Captain Good-hope had
they were sturdy men ; but the captain
ience did also send him some aid, so he
reat. The rest of the armies were hotly
nd the Diabolonians
j j jjjjjjjjjj
@@@@@@@@@@@@@@@@@@@@@@@
???????????????????
%%%%%%%%%%%%%%%%%%%%%%%
QQQQQQQQQQQQQQQQQQQQQQ
RRRRRRRRRRRRRRRRRRRRRR
jiukn tr njhvgftmckgog
cutting and battering shrewdly. Now
engaged, he did stoutly fall on, on
&

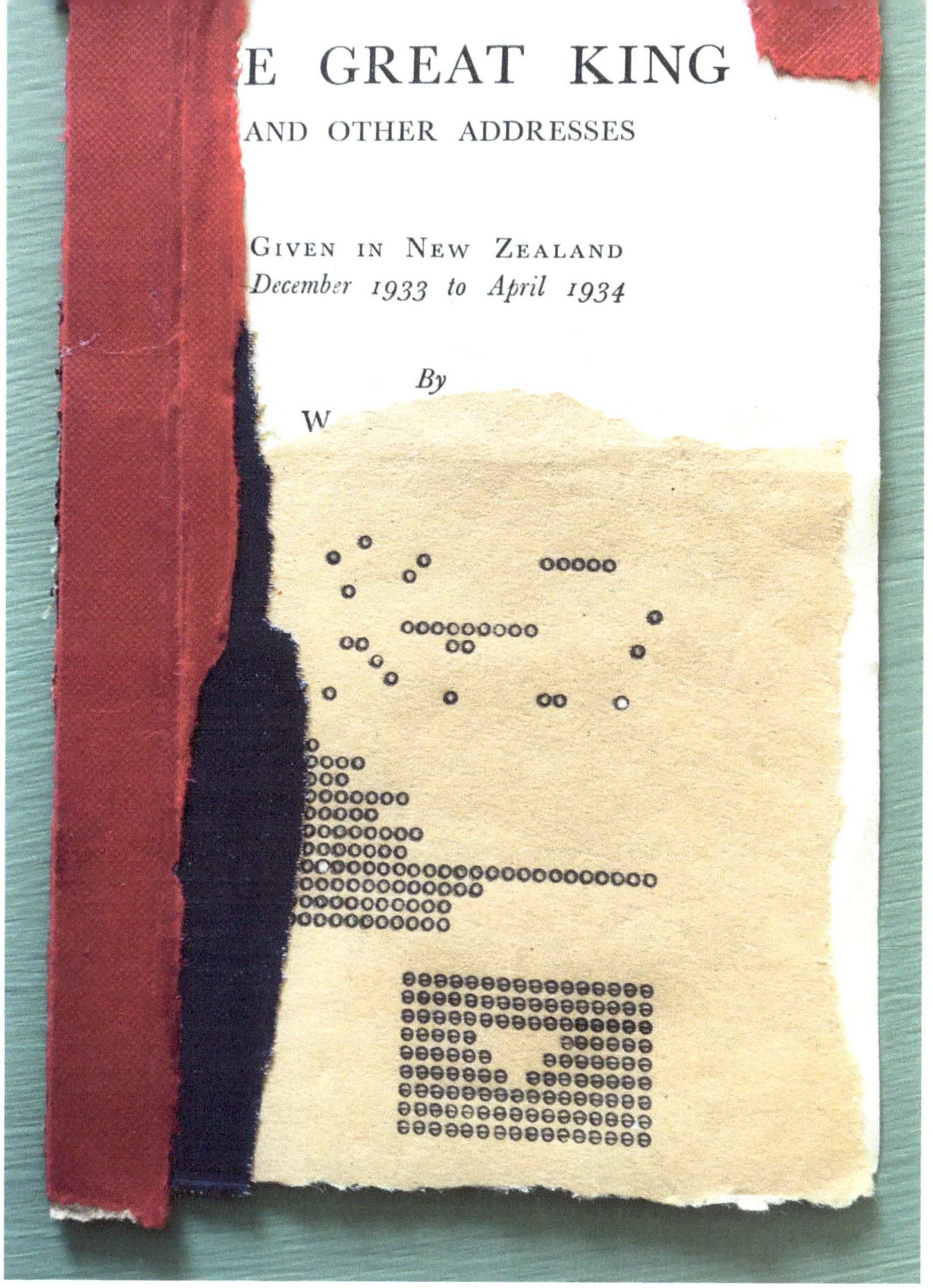
E GREAT KING
AND OTHER ADDRESSES
GIVEN IN NEW ZEALAND
December 1933 to April 1934
By
W

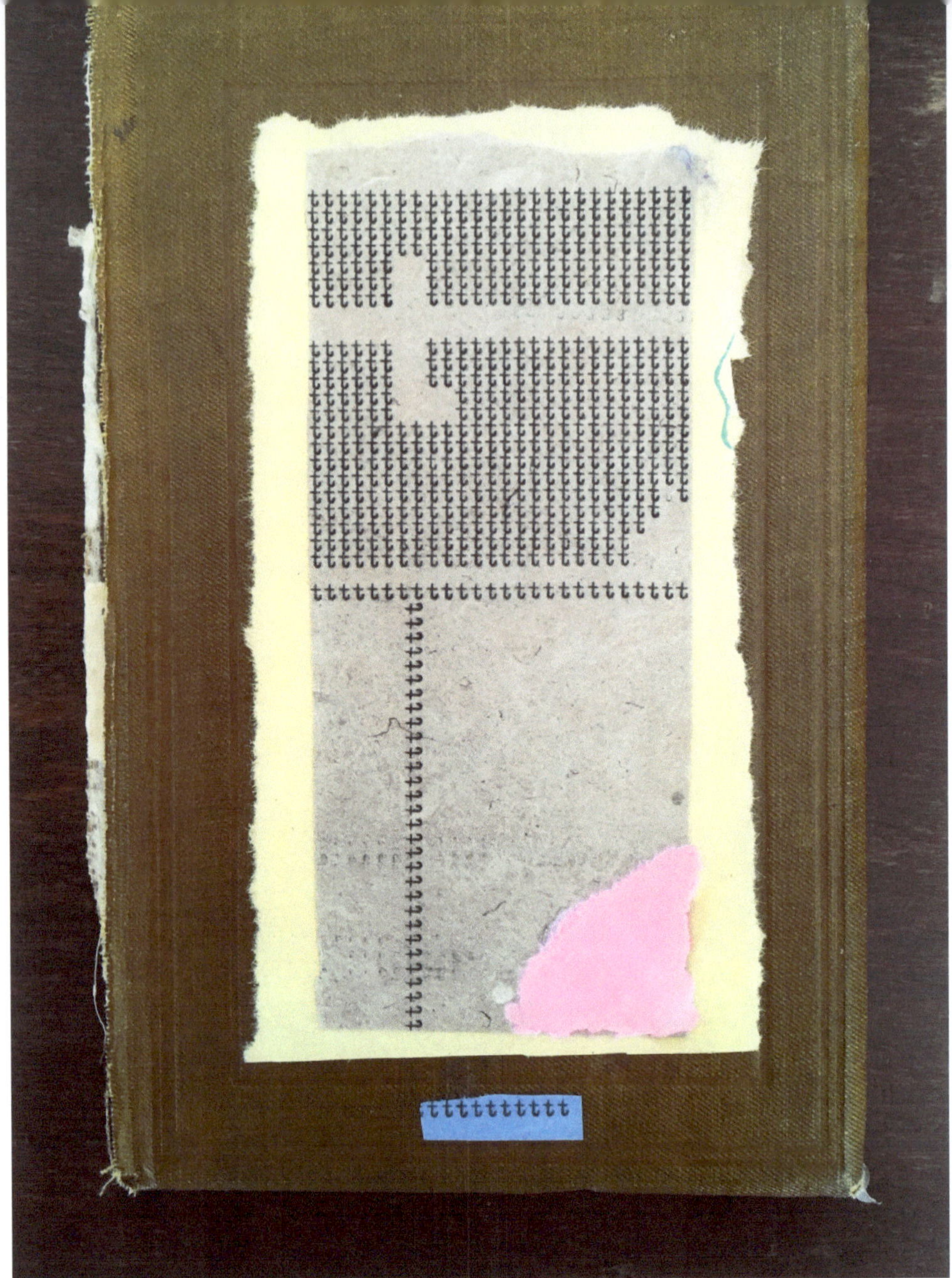

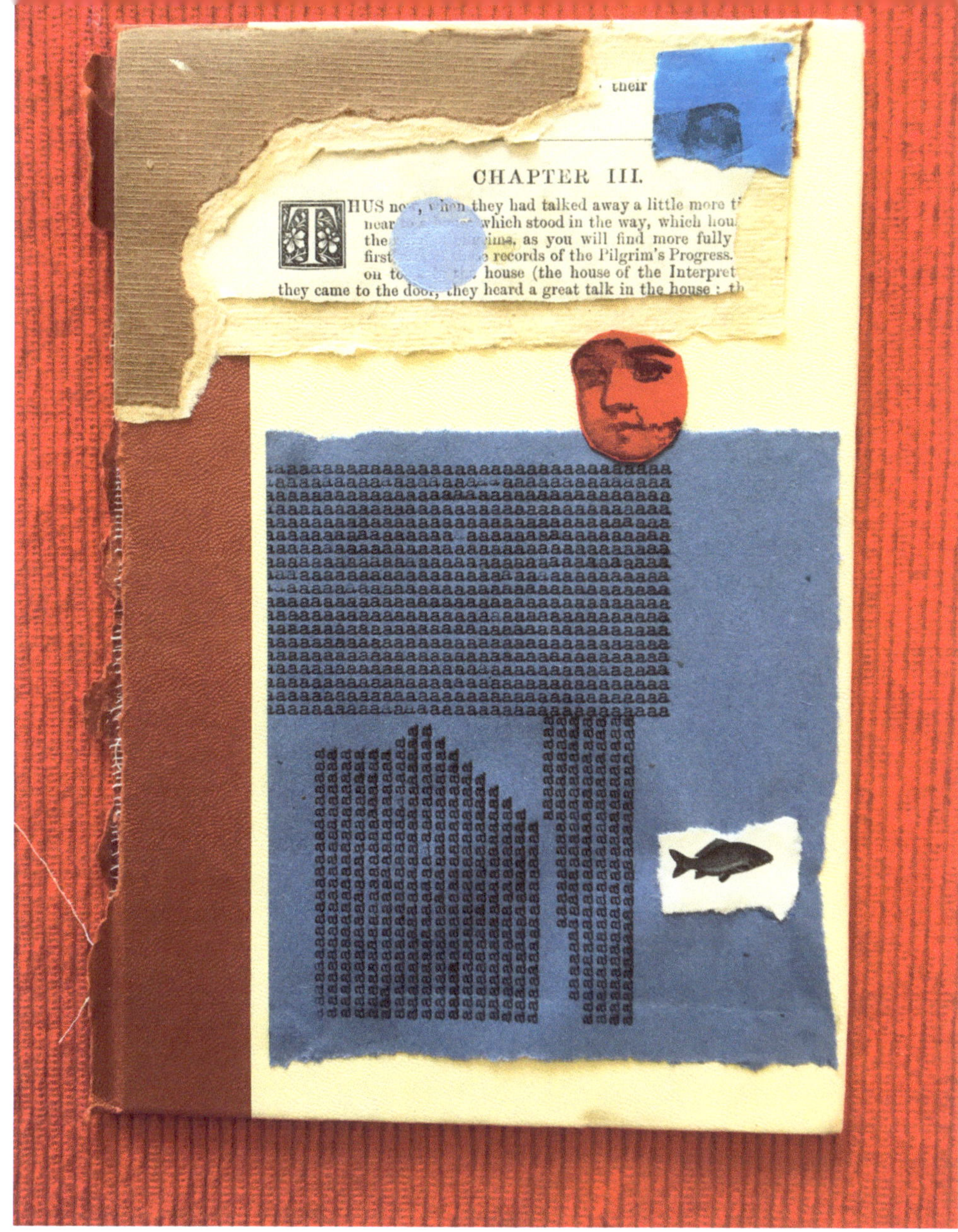
their
CHAPTER III.
they had talked away a little more
which stood in the way, which
as you will find more fully
records of the Pilgrim's Progress.
house (the house of the Interpret
they came to the door, they heard a great talk in the house :

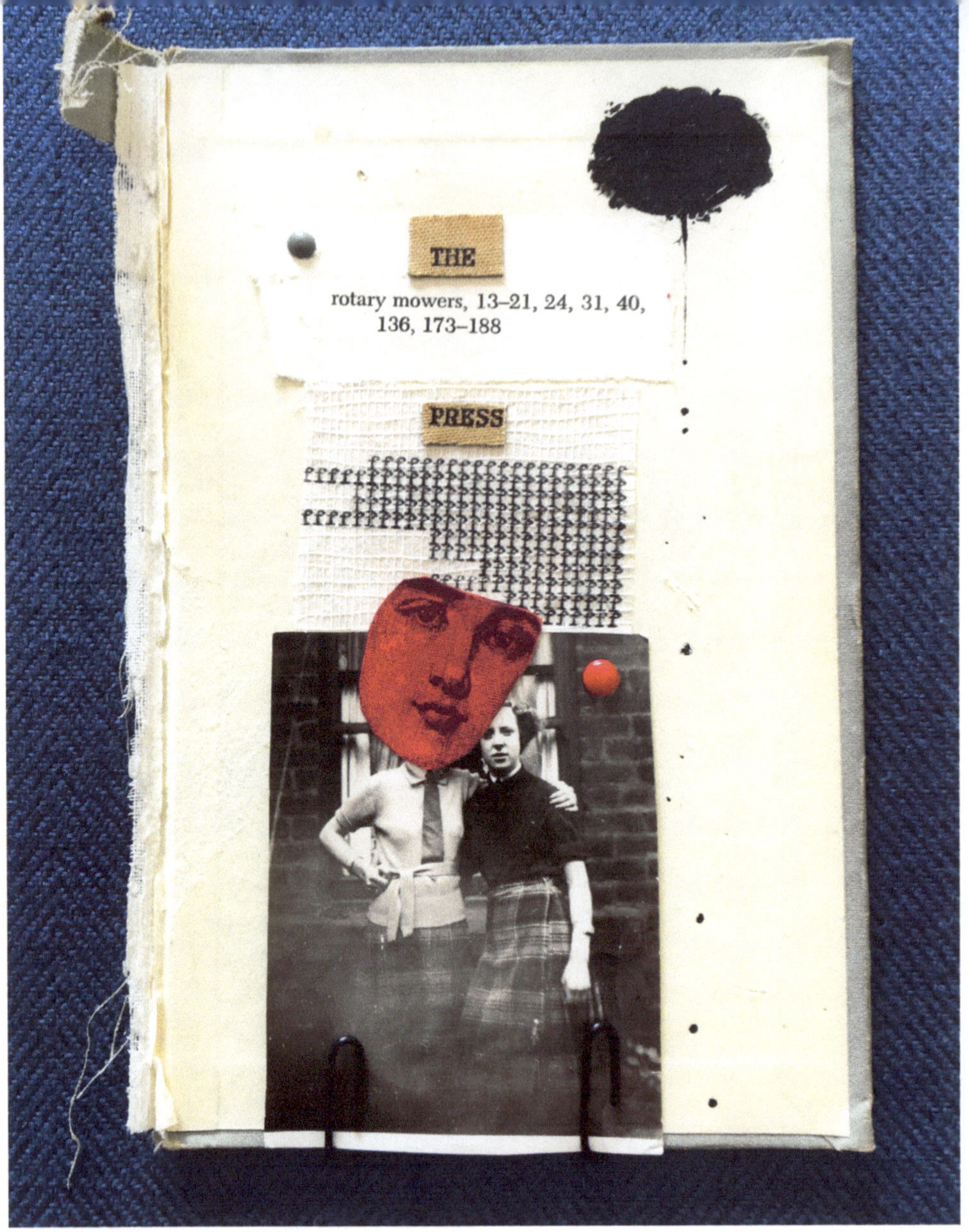
THE
rotary mowers, 13–21, 24, 31, 40,
136, 173–188
PRESS

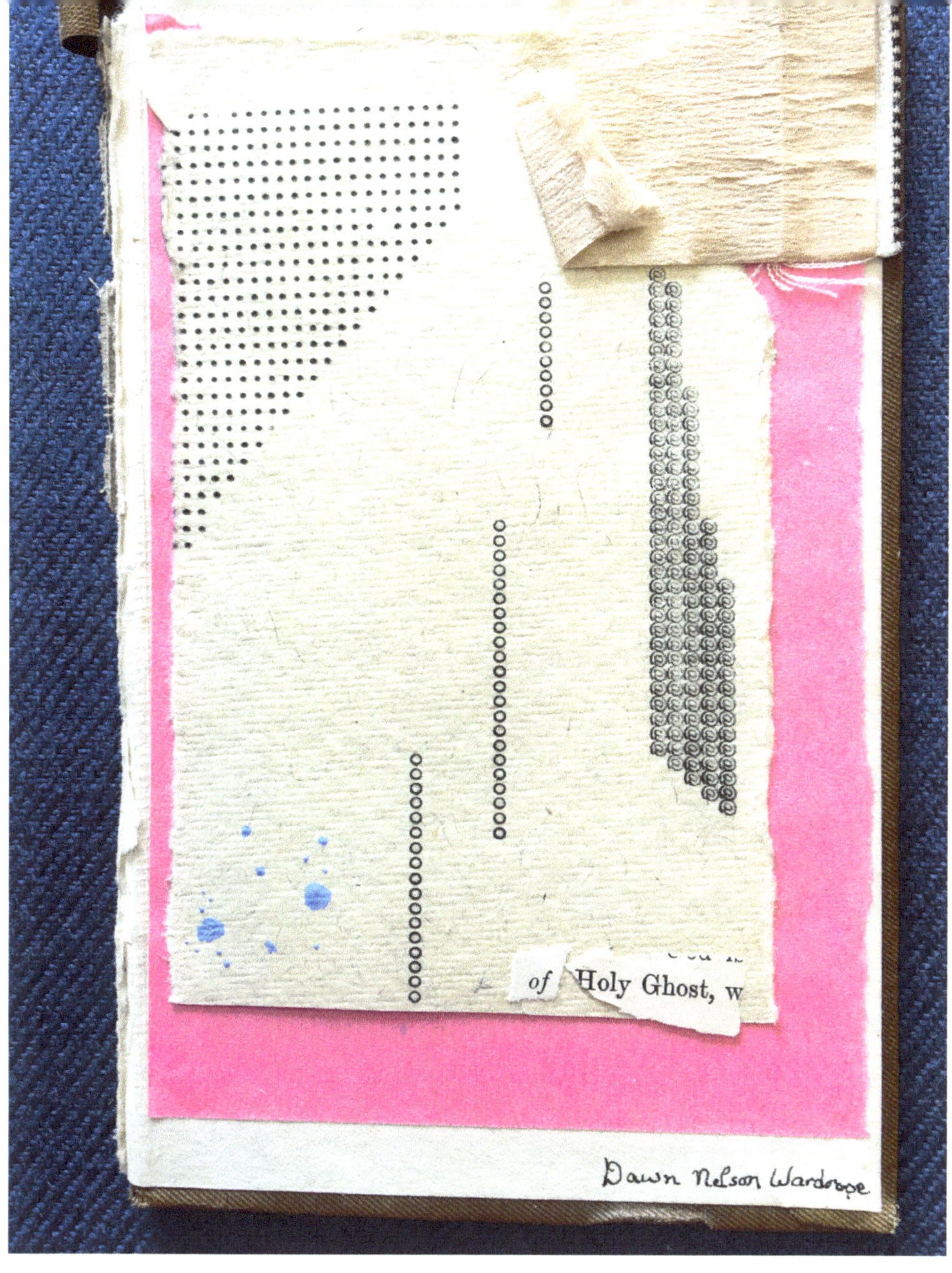
of Holy Ghost, w
Dawn Nelson Wardrope

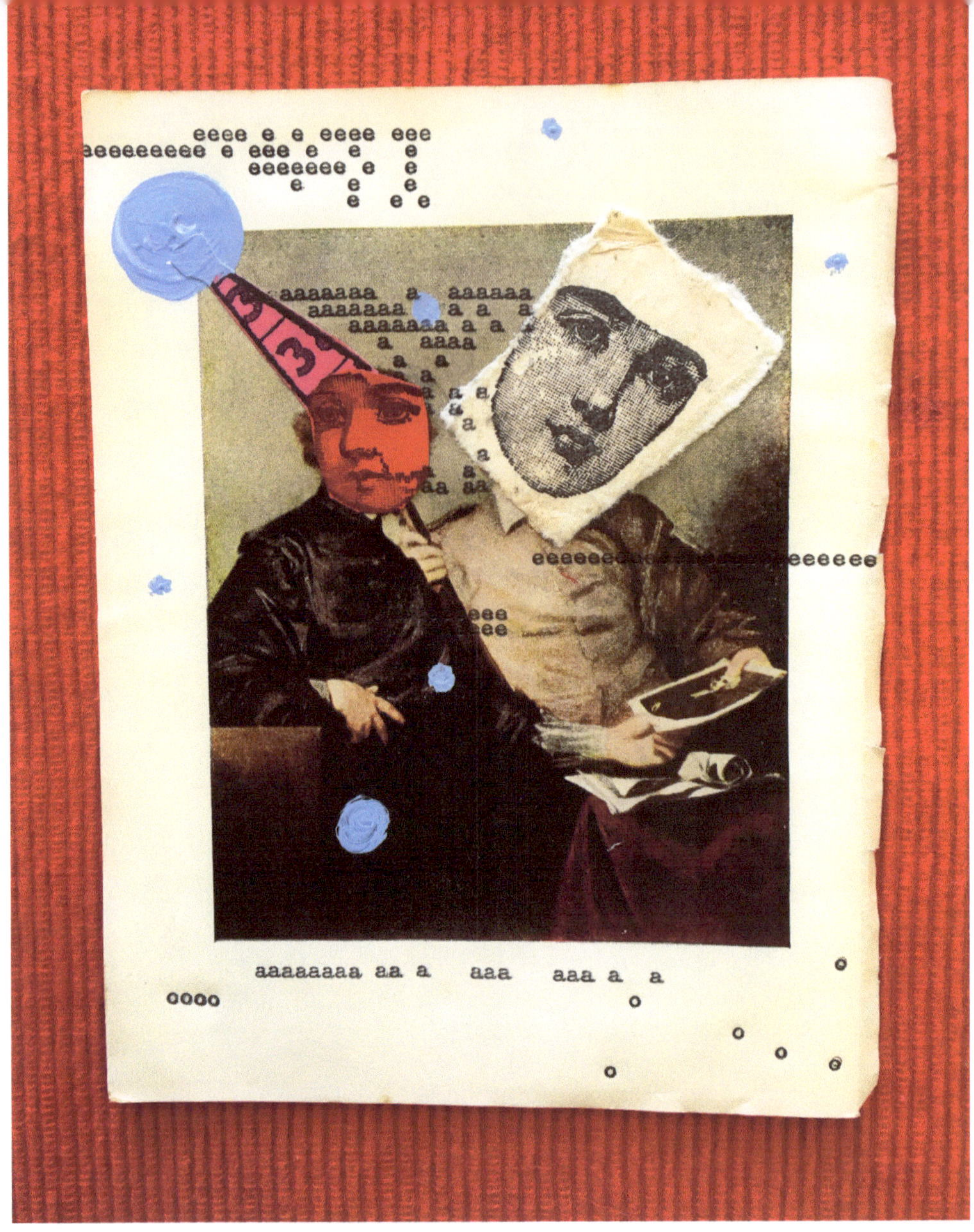

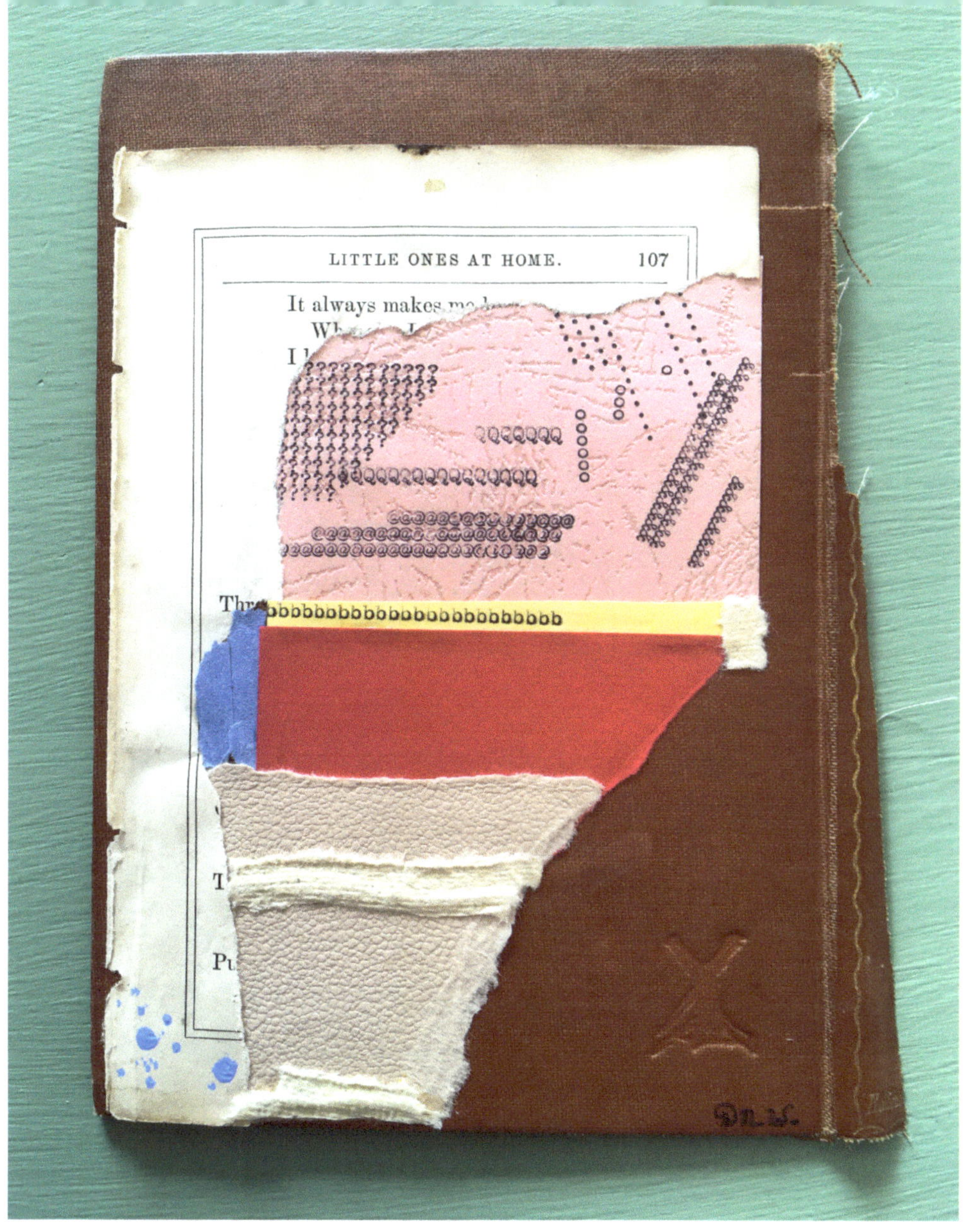
LITTLE ONES AT HOME.
107
It always makes

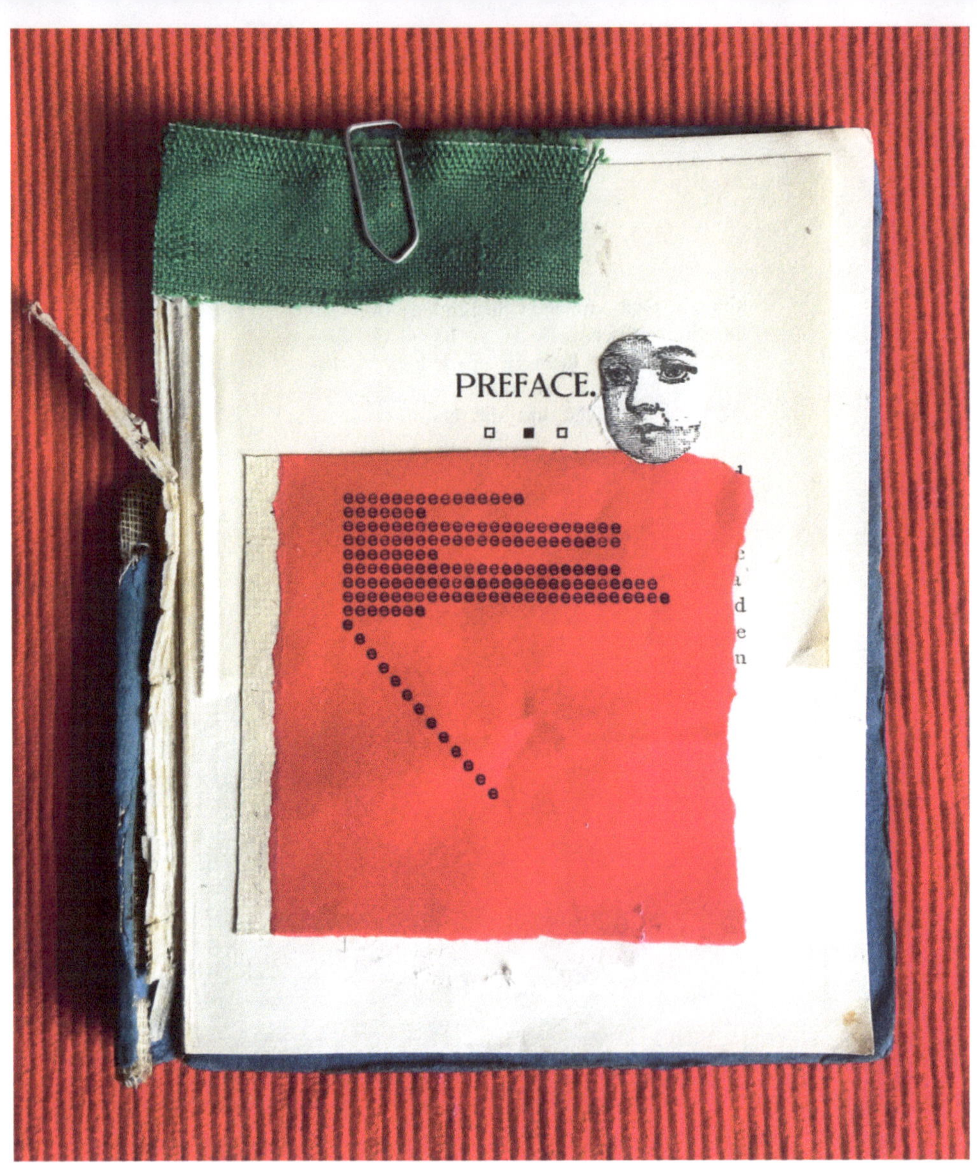
PREFACE.

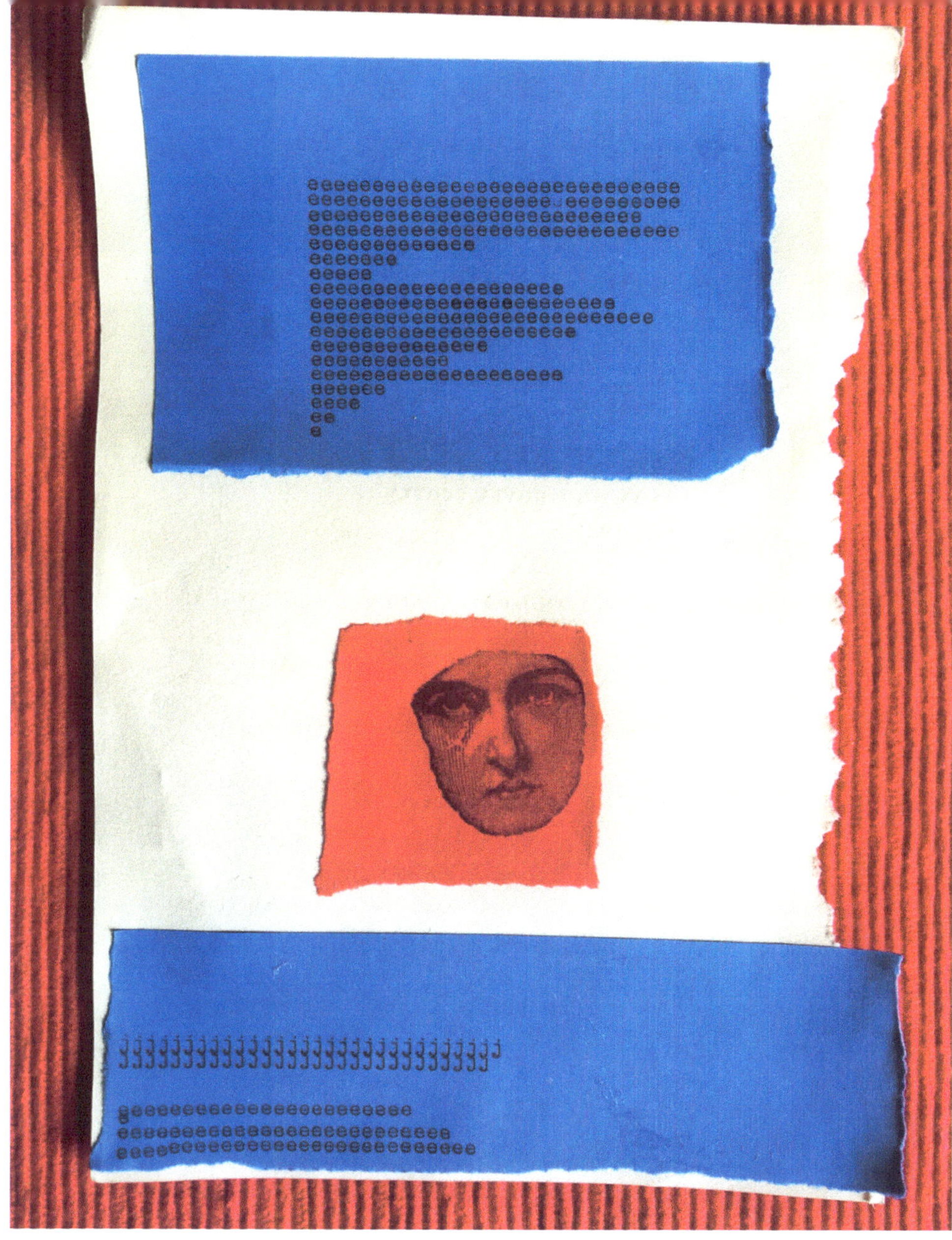

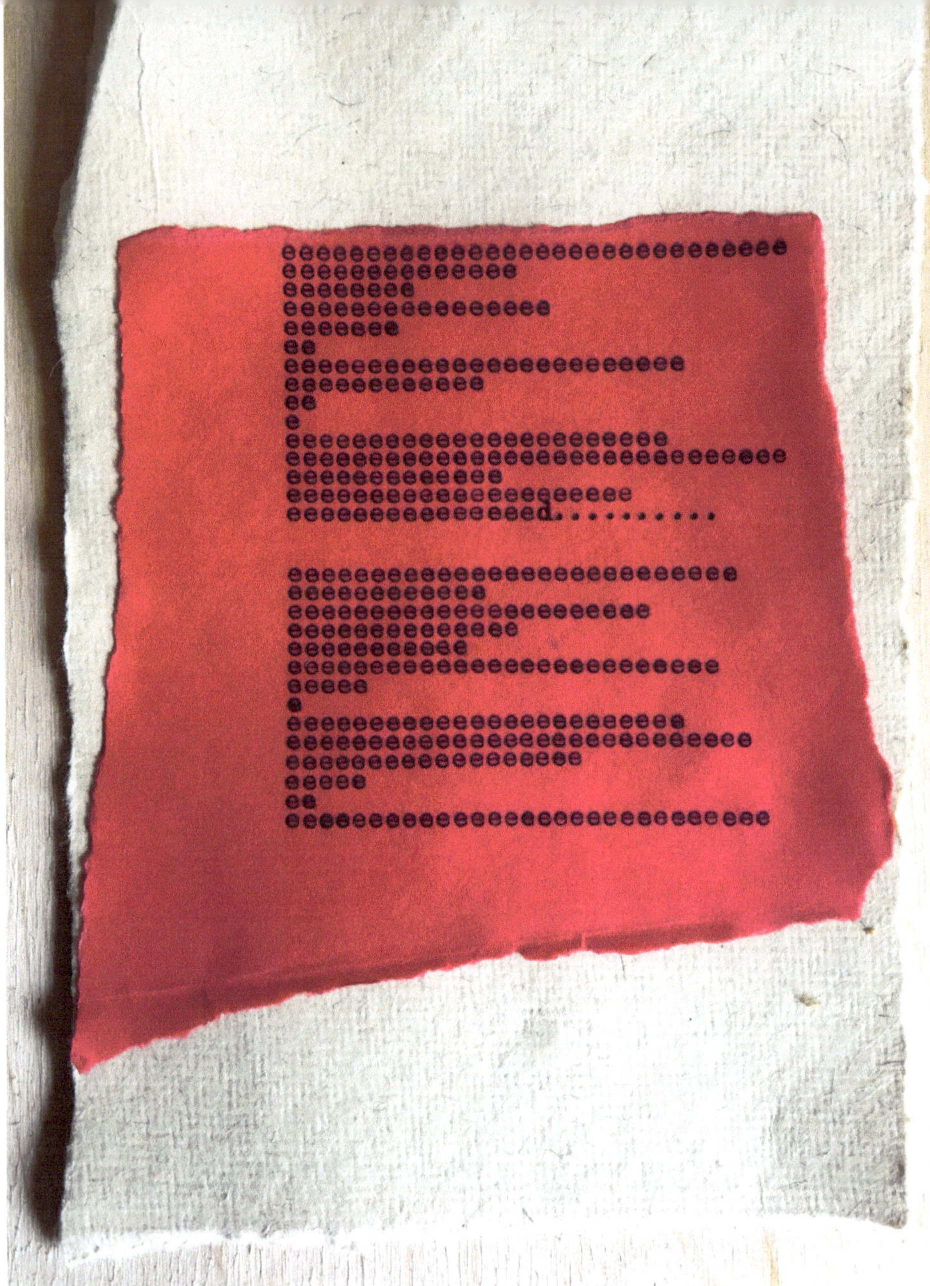
eeeeeeeeeeeeeeeeeeeeeeeeeeeeee
eeeeeeeeeeeeee
eeeeeeee
eeeeeeeeeeeeeeee
eeeeeee
ee
eeeeeeeeeeeeeeeeeeeeeeee
eeeeeeeeeeee
ee
e
eeeeeeeeeeeeeeeeeeeeeee
eeeeeeeeeeeeeeeeeeeeeeeeeeeeee
eeeeeeeeeeeee
eeeeeeeeeeeeeeeeeeeee
eeeeeeeeeeeeeeed..........

eeeeeeeeeeeeeeeeeeeeeeeeeee
eeeeeeeeeeee
eeeeeeeeeeeeeeeeeeeeee
eeeeeeeeeeeeee
eeeeeeeeeee
eeeeeeeeeeeeeeeeeeeeeeeeee
eeeee
e
eeeeeeeeeeeeeeeeeeeeeeee
eeeeeeeeeeeeeeeeeeeeeeeeeeee
eeeeeeeeeeeeeeeeee
eeeee
ee
eeeeeeeeeeeeeeeeeeeeeeeeeeeee

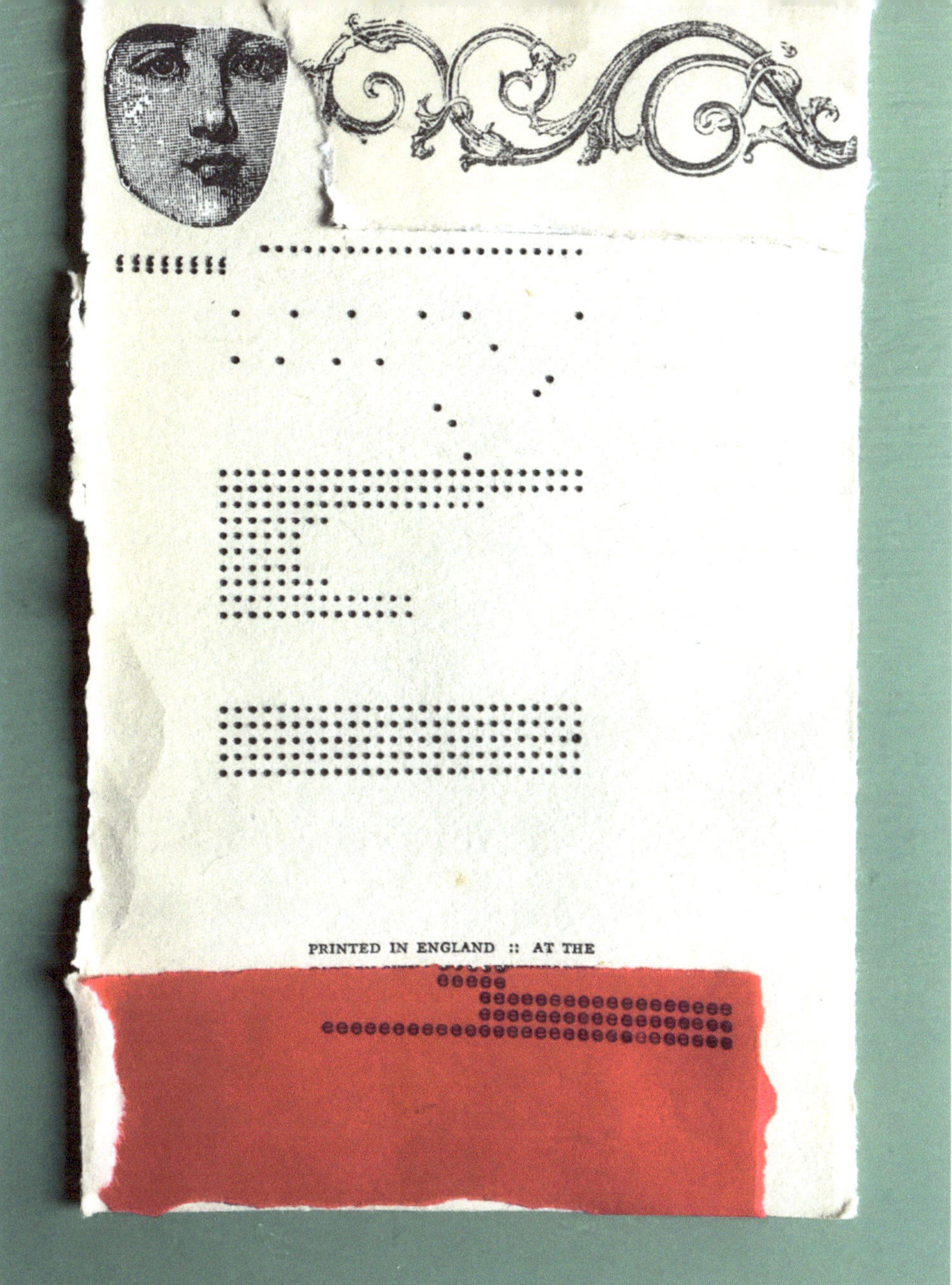
PRINTED IN ENGLAND :: AT THE

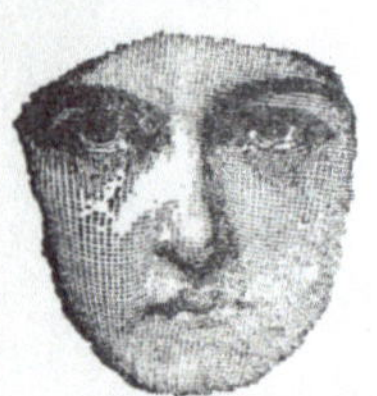
RSE
7: ASPECTS OF
WORK AT THE
METROPOLITAN
TABERNACLE
動の自由をもとめる無産階級の闘争のほうに普選運
とは考えなかったので
前述したコミンテルン第四回大会でつくられた日本共産党綱領草案は、山川の考えと大きく異
なっている。土地の大部分が天皇をはじめとする半封建的大地主の手中にあり、かつ元老が政治
的に重要な役割を占めているような現状では、自由主義的ブルジョアジーも国家権力にたいする
反対勢力となりうる。日本共産党は、過渡的なスローガンとして天皇の政府の転覆と君主制の廃
止をかかげ、かつ普通選挙権獲得の闘争を指導せねばならぬ。そしてこの闘争の指導権をにぎる

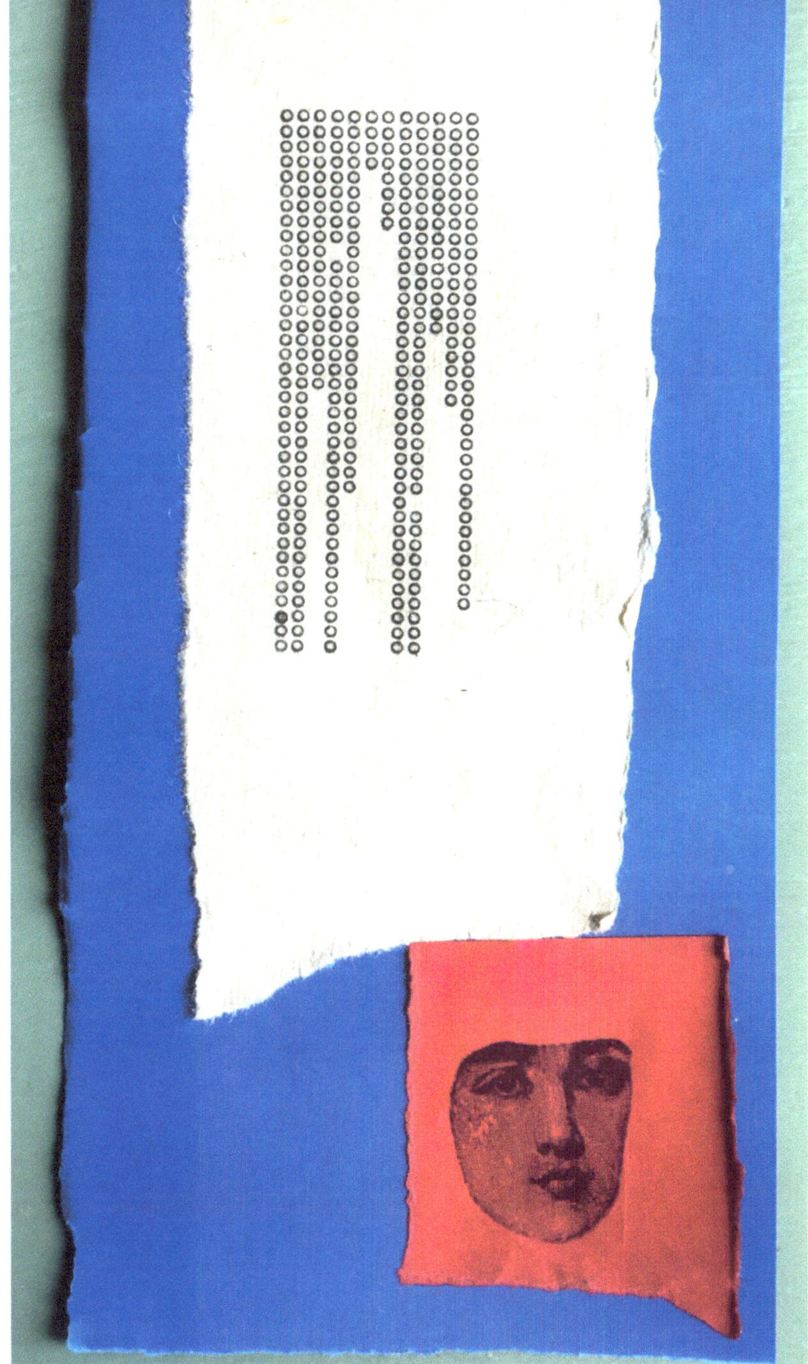

www.ingramcontent.com/pod-product-compliance
Lightning Source LLC
LaVergne TN
LVHW061048110826
845147LV00022B/718
* 9 7 8 1 9 1 2 2 1 1 3 8 8 *